PRAISE FOR

Building a Sustainable
Family Office

"Scott has thoughtfully taken his inspired experience of creating an office and maintaining it and made it accessible to all. I am quite sure that every family who is contemplating creating a family office or transitioning one will benefit from Scott's insights."

—**James (Jay) E. Hughes Jr.**, author of *Family Wealth: Keeping It in the Family* and three other books on family offices

"There is nothing like personal experience and brutal honesty that best teach the opportunities and pitfalls of a family office. Scott has pulled back the curtain so generously and artfully on his family's experience to enlighten us all."

—**Laura Lauder**, Lauder Family Philanthropy Fund

"The book is a great blend of insights based upon Scott's personal experience and work canvassing the space. Whether a veteran or new to the family office challenge/opportunity, one gains grounding as to what's really important."

—**Barney Corning**, counder of the CCC Family Office Alliance

"Saslow's book takes an inherently complex landscape—the family office—and makes it accessible and understandable. With the insider's experience of someone who has built and run a family office, Scott gives step-by-step guidance and practical ideas for how to begin to design, build, or refine an effective family office. This is a must-read for family members and family office professionals alike."

—**Kristin Keffeler,** author of *The Myth of the Silver Spoon: Navigating Family Wealth & Creating an Impactful Life* and *Wealth 3.0: The Future of Family Wealth Advising*

"Scott's book is a testament to the evolving nature of family offices. It offers a blend of theory, practical examples, and strategic advice that speaks directly to wealth owners seeking purpose and impact beyond financial returns."

—**Francois Botha,** *Forbes* contributor on family offices; founder and CEO, Simple

BUILDING A SUSTAINABLE Family Office

AN INSIDER'S GUIDE TO
WHAT WORKS AND WHAT DOESN'T

SCOTT SASLOW

RIVER GROVE
BOOKS

Published by River Grove Books
Austin, TX
www.rivergrovebooks.com

Distributed by River Grove Books

Design and composition by Greenleaf Book Group
Cover design by Greenleaf Book Group

Publisher's Cataloging-in-Publication data is available.

Hardcover ISBN: 978-1-63299-850-7

Paperback ISBN: 978-1-63299-852-1

eBook ISBN: 978-1-63299-851-4

First Edition

For Pops—and all you did on behalf of our family.

CONTENTS

PART 3: SUSTAINING THE FAMILY OFFICE

The author of *Building a Sustainable Family Office* shares his journey of creating his own family office—his observations, memories, and perspectives—and does not represent that these are the same for his parents, spouse, siblings, children, or other relatives. In a few instances, some minor details have been changed to provide privacy for the author, his family, and other colleagues.

Foreword

It is the heart that makes a man rich. He is rich according to what he is, not according to what he has.

—Henry Ward Beecher

I first met Scott Saslow at a CCC Alliance meeting in March of 2018. A few years prior, Scott's family office had joined CCC Alliance, a consortium of single family offices that Barney Corning and I founded in 1994. Scott had recently reengaged with his family office, and as we chatted during a refreshment break, he was candid and thoughtful about the challenges his family was facing. He was also reimagining a new model for his family office. I could empathize with Scott because in 1983, due to a reversed succession plan, I split from a family office founded by my grandfather and his two brothers in 1923. My parents and siblings formed a new family office, and within six years, we were joined by many cousins, aunts, and uncles. The experience of breaking out of a once-sacrosanct family institution was challenging, rewarding, and gut-wrenching, but it paid huge dividends—both financial and psychic.

So, in 2021, when Scott asked me to join an advisory board as he launched his new SFO, I welcomed the opportunity. In moments of hubris, I think I have seen everything in the world of family offices. Between CCC Alliance and the Wharton Global Family Alliance, I have had a window on over 400 SFOs, many of them in launch or reboot mode. However, Scott is an outlier from my experience—that rare person who possesses the technical and interpersonal skills plus the experience of two prior versions at a family office.

A management consultant with a Harvard MBA and an entrepreneur in his own right, Scott exudes humility and is constructively self-critical. Yet the element that keeps the diverse board of ONE WORLD united and motivated is Scott's heart. He is "rich" in kindness and generosity and is an unusual combination of idealism and realism. When Scott identifies a problem or challenge, whether it is within his family enterprise or a thorny global issue, he becomes a tenacious doer. So when Scott informed our board that he was planning to write a book to help families create sustainable family office models, we all took note.

The book you are about to read is unique in the private world of family offices. Granted, the library of books written about family offices is limited. Most of those were authored by consultants, a minority of whom have worked in a family office. Some of these books are helpful, but many are self-promoting. Whether you are a wealth creator planning to launch a family office, a principal, or an executive seeking to make your SFO more sustainable, there are four reasons why Scott's book is an important resource. First, it is written from the perspective of a family principal, and as any family executive will tell you, the family principal is the ultimate decision-maker and bears the long-term financial and familial consequences. Family offices that endure over many generations focus as much on family capital as they do on financial capital.

Second, Scott highlights his own successes and failures, and these mistakes are highly instructive. A multigenerational family office I know routinely shares what their fifth generation now refers to as "fail tales" as powerful learning tools. Third, Scott has no underlying product or service to sell. (Except perhaps this book, which I assume you have already purchased.) Over the past two decades, the family office market has grown from an arcane niche to what is now viewed as a sticky, high-margin market. In the opaque world of service providers, you need to be cognizant of how your advisors are compensated. Finally, this book is written with humility, and anyone who has raised a family, dealt with adolescents, marriage, divorce, and aging parents knows how humbling it can be. Now add wealth and overseeing the family office into the mix, and you have a bigger, albeit high-class, challenge.

Ego is a great destroyer of family wealth, and we are all familiar with those who have made a great fortune and suddenly believe they have the secret of success in all aspects of life, only to lose both the assets and family relationships. I believe the dour Scottish philosopher Thomas Carlyle said it best: "Adversity is sometimes hard upon a man; but for one man who can stand prosperity, there are a hundred that will stand adversity."

Laird Pitcairn Pendleton
Cofounder, CCC Alliance LLC
Boston, Massachusetts
2024

Introduction

"Are you familiar with the Challenger 300?" The question startled me as I was looking out the window of the plane and onto the tarmac, gazing at other jets and wondering which was Sergey's or Larry's. The rumor was that they had invested in this private airport facility in Silicon Valley that I was about to take off from—in a Challenger 300.

"Yes, I'm familiar. Thank you. I'll get my seat belt on."

With that click of the buckle, it all started to become more real, even the unreal parts of this day. I was the only passenger on a private jet about to travel from the Bay Area to Florida, with a stopover in the Midwest so that my siblings could hop in. We were traveling to visit my father, who was likely a few weeks from passing. It was also the middle of a global pandemic, when most travel of all types had halted. Oh, and I was going to Florida of all places. Though it's normally a very pleasant place to visit, Florida in the winter of 2020 was experiencing one of the largest spikes in COVID cases in the country.

Just a few weeks earlier, on a chilly and overcast Saturday in November, I was in the checkout line at the Ace Hardware a few blocks from my home in California with my twelve-year-old daughter. She and I were working on a project to create a giant homemade foosball table requiring some new wooden rods. Waiting in line for a register to open up, I glanced down at my cell to see who was calling. It was my father, and that was a red flag. Speaking with him was a regular weekly occurrence—but it was always on Sundays. Something was not right, and I was a bit concerned, so I answered.

"Hi, Dad. Everything okay?"

"Yeah, all okay. Are you somewhere we can talk?"

Not good. "Let me call you when I am back home," I said.

When I called back fifteen minutes later, he said, "Look, I just want to let you know that I am going to be stopping my dialysis, and . . ."

My father had had kidney cancer twenty years earlier, and a remarkable surgeon at the Cleveland Clinic had artfully removed a portion of one of his kidneys, which allowed him many years of good living. Then, about five years ago, the first kidney failed completely, and the second one was not doing so well, so he had started dialysis. Now, with his general health failing, he decided it was time to stop and enjoy his last few weeks without tubes, tests, and blood draws. He said he thought it would be a good idea for me and my siblings to come and visit him. What he didn't need to say was that this would be our last visit.

This was in early December 2020, and for the history buffs out there, it was still the early stages of the coronavirus pandemic; the world was in a most unsettled place, to put it lightly. My poor aging father, off of his dialysis and very immunocompromised, was living in a region with one of the highest numbers of coronavirus cases. I booked my flight immediately.

I had brought a journal for writing my thoughts down during the six-hour flight. On it I wrote three questions:

- What am I going to experience these next few days?

- What will be the same once my father is gone?

- What will be different?

My father was a sharp and successful businessman, and he was my hero in many ways. He always came up with a creative solution to most problems and could read a room beautifully. This was perhaps due to his military training; he had been an intelligence officer stationed in Korea for a few years right out of college. Over the years, I could go to him for any issue large or small. He was remarkable at remembering the important events in my life—what was up at my work, how my wife or kids were faring in their specific interests. He was also the initial source of wealth for my family. Dad taught me the best he could how to take care of my business, my wealth, and my family. He and I had this saying, "Ojos abiertos," which loosely translates in Spanish to "eyes open"—a reminder to pay attention, to always be on the ball.

Within a couple of weeks, I realized, I would be losing him as a guiding light, and what I did with my life would truly rest on my shoulders. I'd be accountable only to myself, and also fully accountable for the wealth he had created and passed on to my family line. And to make matters more complicated, our family was in an unstable transition period with our family office, the business entity that cared for our family's accrued wealth. For several years, we had worked with an external (nonfamily) office manager, hired to create and manage our family office. The last few months had been quite complicated; we were working on a new model of support from the manager, with the added challenge of some family members pulling capital out from the centralized structure. In short, there were a lot of moving parts and uncertainty as we tried to put this new structure in place.

Back on the tarmac in San Jose, CA, it was almost time for takeoff. I was starting the highly emotional journey of losing my father and the highly challenging journey of rebuilding my family office.

I flew to Florida on a Monday. Exactly one week later, my father passed peacefully, with my stepmother at his side. Approximately two weeks after that, the family received a resignation letter from our family office manager. As bad as the situation was—the emotional upheaval and sadness of losing my father together with the simultaneous family office uncertainty—my siblings and I knew we had to act quickly.

When you are part of a wealthy family, even if you create a career path that is separate from the family business or family office, at some point, you can't ignore the wealth. Believe me, I tried. For the first part of my career, I was keen to work in the technology sector and was employed in fascinating organizations helping to bring the internet and software into the mainstream. I later built a business in the leadership development field. I loved my work, in part because I worked hard to create it on my own. As family capital became available to me later in my career, I was certainly grateful for the position I was in and yet still kept that part of my life separate from my day job, at least for a while. After all, I didn't think I'd earned the funds, and I didn't think I was responsible for them, but I was.

I have been a principal in my family's family office for the last twenty years, the last five of which involved me rebuilding my family line's family office. This was a huge undertaking, and even with the best consultants and providers, I wish I'd had a book such as this one. I have spoken with dozens of other family principals who don't feel they are as engaged with their family office as they can be, don't feel as knowledgeable as they would like to be, and don't feel their family office is meeting their needs. In many instances, family offices ultimately break apart, causing pain for the families and the broader society that benefits from the offices' investing and philanthropic activities.

My intent in sharing my own story and what I've learned is to help other principals hear in detail, in an open and honest way, how another family office started, grew, and was rebuilt a few times. I want to share with you, the reader, not only what I did but also how I was thinking through the issue. Each family—and, therefore, each family office—is unique, yet some of the themes are universal. I hope that, by sharing my story, I help others think about where they are in relation to their own office.

Managing a family office requires a unique management paradigm. You may think that building the office is simple (after all, many family office principals are experts at running operating companies), or that you can just hire an outside manager to take care of the office and call it done. That is not the case. Principals in many family offices spend the bulk of their energy and time in the mechanical area of investing—which is certainly necessary but not at all sufficient. Properly and purposefully designing the family office is a critical first stage. Without the right mindset and the proper underlying structure, even the best manager will struggle to keep a family office afloat. Even then, the family office is not a discrete activity that can be left alone; it's a living organism that must be cared for. You'll need to sustain the office and evolve with the times and with your family's needs.

There are around ten thousand family offices in the world, and half of those have been created in the last decade. They control a disproportionate amount of wealth—approximately $6 trillion—more than all hedge funds combined. It is estimated that 40 percent of those family offices will fail to successfully pass the family's accrued wealth down to the next generation. There is a pervasive global pattern of wealthy families moving from shirtsleeve to shirtsleeve—or rags to riches and back to rags, if you like—in three generations. This short tenure sets the family back, but it also deprives broader society of the benefits it would otherwise receive from philanthropy and investing. Clearly, what's being done in many offices is not working.

My research, as well as my own experience, points to a new management paradigm as a solution for sustaining the family office. This approach takes many cues from running other types of operating companies but similarly recognizes the unique elements of the family office. It starts with the mindset of the principals: how they view the challenge at hand, how they see their own role, and how they think about defining a collaborative purpose. Of course, it's also crucial they make the proper investments and learn how to develop talent—within both the family and the broader ecosystem of providers. Properly addressing the unique business and personal realities of a family office will increase its effectiveness and help sustain the family office for years.

COVID, my father's passing, and the changing of the guard in the family office—all combined to create one of the most stressful times in my life. My siblings and I, all with different levels of business expertise, had to converge and work as a team to rebuild our family office. We compressed what might optimally be a multiyear process into a couple of quarters, and we ended up with what is a solid new family office structure. The experience took some years off my life, but we had a great team of professionals working alongside us. I promised myself that, if I made it out in one piece, I'd write a book to help others. So here's that book.

PART 1

DESIGNING THE FAMILY OFFICE

The roots of a sustainable family office start well before the office actually exists. It is crucial that the office first begin with an understanding of who it serves, what it does, and why. It is important to set your family up for success early. A sustainable family office will require a purpose beyond simply managing wealth. That might mean philanthropy or travel, support for the family business or a life of leisure, but it works best when the purpose is uniquely suited to your family and when it is thoughtfully crafted and communicated openly across the family. That purpose needs to align with the family's collective values and visions for the future. With a purpose in place, you can design a structure for the family office that will allow it to function effectively, provided you also design an effective leadership team and manage their performance toward the office's goals.

Talking to your children about their financial future—and planning for that future—are integral aspects of preparing for sustainability. We also need to understand what the family office does for your family and even who constitutes family. We need to prepare the next generation for running the family office and the family business, through education, business experience, accountability, and even guardrails to keep them from destroying their inheritance in a few years. And we need to understand the purpose, a vision for the future, and the values the family office will be based on. Like building a house, a well-planned, solid structure is fundamental as well, and the leadership you offer or hire for your family office can make all the difference. With all these pieces in place, you are set up to design a family office that will see your family through many generations and achieve your desired impact on the broader society.

CHAPTER 1

What Is a Family Office?

Our family's wealth origin story starts with a German immigrant named Hugo Friedman who came to the United States in the late 1800s to find a better life for his family. In Germany, he had been a craftsman, a maker of medical instruments. Upon his arrival in the US, he moved to the Midwest and, in 1908, set up his own shop to manufacture these same products and sell them to larger distribution companies. His business plodded along for many decades, not growing significantly but providing a steady income for his wife and two children. Fast-forward to 1958, and my father, the younger of those two sons of immigrant parents from Europe, had finished college, served two years in Korea as a counterintelligence officer for the US military, and was looking for a small company to purchase. He found one that had a great reputation for quality, and the founder was looking to sell and retire. The stars aligned for my father to purchase the business for around $100,000.

My father enjoyed running the business and making continuous improvements. In concert with the US's economic growth from the 1960s onward, he grew the business year after year. By the time I was born, in 1972, the last of three children, the family business was nicely profitable and growing each year. As any member of a family with its own business knows, the lines between the family and the business are often blurred. Just from the dinner conversations about my father's day, my siblings and I were exposed to important leadership concepts over the years. My siblings and I enjoyed attending company picnics and holiday parties. My father would often bring his executive team to our home and have his offsites at our kitchen table. As a kid growing up and into high school, I loved meeting these company leaders; they were friendly and laid back and always made my siblings and me feel welcome to listen in to the conversation while we made our after-school snacks in the kitchen.

The family business was growing steadily each year. While my father never discussed how much money the family had, he worked with estate professionals to pass this money down to us. All along through his career, since early in his days at the family business, he set money aside for us. And due to the power of compounding interest, assets can grow nicely if given enough time. Eventually, he had accumulated enough wealth that he needed to actively manage it, and he created a family office structure embedded in the family business.

A family office is just what it sounds like—and not at all what it sounds like at the same time. It's an office for the family—not a room in which the family works but a constellation of business entities, investment vehicles, along with internally hired professionals and a network of outsourced professionals who all work on behalf of the family. Some offices serve just one or a few family members, and they may be exclusively focused on managing investment capital and interacting with outside accountants and attorneys. Although it is rare, some family offices span three, four, or five generations, serve hundreds of family members, and have more than a hundred professionals managing hundreds of legal entities and providing a wide variety of wealth management, philanthropy, and other concierge services, such as coordinating travel and leisure activities.

The family office's structure and function are often unique, catering to the individual needs of a particular family. The family's involvement—who makes decisions and who benefits—can also vary widely from family to family and even among family members. However, the general purpose of the family office is the same: maintaining and growing a family's assets through the generations so the family members, as well as the business they control and the philanthropic endeavors they support, can benefit from it.

Although it is crucial to build the family office for your specific needs, identifying those needs begins with understanding who will benefit from the office's services. Defining family is harder than it sounds. You'll also need to be absolutely clear about what your family office is—defining the office part of family office. Is it an extension of your family's operating business (if one exists) or a stand-alone entity with a singular focus? Perhaps most important is that the family office grows and evolves with your family's needs.

Who counts as family?

The first crucial aspect of a family office is determining which family members are part of it and, most critically, whether they will participate in the office and receive the services it offers equally. Not only are these critical questions to address, they are critical to ask up front in the process of creating a new office or refreshing an existing office. After all, as bespoke organizations, family offices need to be clear on who they serve and how the members will interact with the entity.

According to Raphael Amit, a management professor at The Wharton School, a lack of shared aspirations across family members can pull the office apart over time. Professor Amit, who cofounded, along with Laird

Pendleton, and leads the Wharton Global Family Alliance, believes that it is most important to clarify who is supported by the family office and to be transparent about what that coverage amounts to, both vertically—through the generations, including grandparents, children, stepchildren—and horizontally—among the principals, their spouses, domestic partners, stepsiblings, and ex-spouses. Professor Amit believes that to preserve harmony among family members and financial prosperity, it is important to clarify the range of services that are provided by the family office and the ways in which the costs of operating the family office are allocated to each family member who is supported by the family office. Last, Professor Amit highlights the crucial role of family office governance and decision-making processes. If this process is unclear, it may be seen as unfair and may breed resentment, pulling at the seams of the office.

When you build or refurbish your own family office, you will have to decide for yourselves who it represents. The original creator of wealth is the starting point, but there are many potential roles that an individual may play relative to that person, which may warrant including them in the office.

We can separate members like a family tree, by generations. The first is the wealth creator themselves, which we often designate as G1, for generation 1. G1 also includes the spouse or partner of the wealth creator or the initial partner in the event of death, divorce, or separation. Subsequent spouses might also be included in G1, as well as the extended family of the wealth creator: siblings, parents, cousins.

The second generation (G2) includes the children (and sometimes but not always stepchildren) of the wealth creator and their spouse, partner, and in some cases, G2 ex-spouses, especially if they have children with the G2 principals. The children of G2 family members are therefore part of G3, and so on.

With this understanding, we have the universe of potential members of the family office from a beneficiary standpoint, meaning those who formally own and control assets and also those who benefit from them.

These beneficiaries may receive income and dividends of financial assets or may utilize nonfinancial family assets such as vacation property, aircraft, and so on. In many cases, the direct descendants of the wealth creator are the primary beneficiaries of the assets, and there are restrictions on how nonfamily members (in-laws and stepchildren) can participate in family assets.

Similarly, there is a variety of protocols for if and how family members can work in the family office and its related entities. Some families choose to primarily look to family members to run family businesses and other family assets; some have explicit policies that exclude family members from serving in full-time operating roles in the family-owned business, and all variations in between are possible. My company has conducted research on this topic and found that a sizable proportion of spouses and even family members over twenty-five years of age are not encouraged to be part of the family office.[1]

Across the different members of the family office, you will also need to determine who receives which privileges from the office, who has which rights and responsibilities, and yes, who receives which assets. A family office usually designates principals, who are the principal beneficiaries and decision-makers of the office. Principals are the owners of the capital; often, this follows the bloodline from the original creator of the wealth, as it did in my family.

However, when G2—my siblings and me—brought domestic partners, who subsequently became spouses, into the picture, things changed. My father, following the best practices of the time from various estate attorneys, made it pretty clear that company shares and the liquid assets those shares kicked off via distributions were for the immediate family only by putting such shares into trusts for the benefit of the family members. As is common in family offices, prenuptial agreements clarified that in the event of divorce, the shares remained tied to the immediate family member, not the spouse.

Beyond this technical arrangement, what was the emotional arrangement that G2 spouses endured? In my case, and with my wife, it was at times very challenging. For example, when my father would want to update my siblings and me on a family office matter, he'd make it clear that spouses were not part of the conversation. The entire family might be on a holiday vacation, at the family vacation property, or at my father's home, and my father would request that just my siblings and I sequester ourselves in a separate room for an hour or two. My wife was surprised and hurt not to be included, even as an observer. This exclusion immediately made it clear, at least in her mind, that there was a two-tier system at play and that she was in the lower tier.

In retrospect, I should have done a better job explaining what such meetings were about and why it was decided that only my siblings and I would attend. Perhaps since I didn't really see the reason or wisdom for restricting these meetings, I didn't feel equipped to explain that to my wife. These incidents would only happen once or twice a year, but because they would happen at nearly every get-together, my wife (and perhaps other in-laws) developed a bit of a fear of going to any family gathering. It also affected my relationship with my wife; I had to defend this practice, yet I wasn't sure I thought it was the best practice myself. But did I have a clear idea of an alternative way the family could have handled things? No, I didn't. Perhaps had we clearly defined family and communicated transparently that spouses of G2 get certain rights and have certain responsibilities different from those of the G2 family principals, this could have been less of a problem. With the rules set in advance and applied to all parties the same (e.g., G2 spouses treated the same), I could have more easily explained the situation, even if I didn't agree with it. You will always have people who might not love the rules themselves, but at least if those rules are laid out in advance, they won't be taken personally.

Determining who is considered family may be easier said than done, but it must be done. If G1 is still around, it is often the case of the golden rule: "He who has the gold makes the rules." G1 and, likely, their spouse will weigh heavily into the decision process in situations where the office is being created for the first time. G2 may be involved, depending on their age; G2s in their midtwenties or later are more likely to be involved in the decision-making process, to the extent that G1 is open to such collaboration. Even in cases when G2 or later is setting up the office, they may refer back to G1's desires—stated or implied—around who receives family wealth. Typically, for family business shares (as opposed to liquid wealth in the form of stocks, etc.), it is even more likely that there are stipulations written into the family business governance documents on who can receive shares of the company, should one owner pass.

A clear definition of family is a guiding light in making potentially contentious decisions. It can help provide answers to difficult questions such as determining the inheritance when one generation passes. It can help you determine, for example, who will run the family foundation when the current leader has stepped down. It can clarify who will make decisions on how funds are invested or how withdrawals work or who has use of the family vacation property.

The role of elders is also an issue that needs to be addressed in the process of defining family: Who gets which roles and responsibilities? For example, you may want to require that when a principal reaches sixty-five years of age, they pass along specified operating roles to younger principals yet may remain part of the board.

While it can be challenging for the decision-makers (be they just one or several across a generation) to determine which family members receive what rights and responsibilities, it is best to be open about the rationale and to try to define roles early in the process (e.g., before G2 or G3 gets married or has children). In this way, the process is more utilitarian and less personal.

What kind of office?

In the same way that you need to carefully define family, you need to carefully define office. How institutional of an entity do you want to build? How many checks and balances should be put in place? How similar to an operating business should it be in terms of structures and processes?

A family office is quite different from a family-controlled business, and, as such, it needs a unique management framework. A family business, if it is still held within the family, offers a service or product to customers; the family office may also offer services, but they are intended for the family's direct benefit. Those services might include financial advice and planning, tax services and accounting, legal representation, support for philanthropy, and a multitude of other services. The family office offers exclusive services for a unique customer set. Yet many families make the mistake of thinking the entities can be managed similarly to the family business and sometimes by the same key individuals.

The family business is often managed to deliver a great service and product, and to maximize profits. The family office takes care of administrative functions for the family. For some, the office is viewed as a cost center, and the mentality is to invest the minimum amount of time and energy—just enough to get the basic functions completed. Yet successful and sustainable family offices have top-quality professional talent that are appropriate for the task at hand; formal governance practices, similar to an operating company; and play an important role in helping the principals reach their vision for their current work and future legacy.

Family members' involvement in either organization can vary. However, the family business is typically run by a subset of the family. Rarely does every member have an operating role. The family office, on the other hand, tends to serve every family member—at least everyone you've defined as part of the core family. It is common for the older generations to maintain certain decision-making powers until the subsequent generation is in their forties or later.

Family businesses are typically highly professionalized, especially in larger and profitable, growing entities. Within family offices, the level of professionalism varies significantly; some are highly professional, and others are resource deprived. In either type of organization, how well the organization is run determines how long it lasts. A family office that is underfunded or treated as an afterthought or side project is unlikely to last beyond one or two generations.

Table 1.1. Comparison of a Family Business to a Family Office

	FAMILY BUSINESS	FAMILY OFFICE
Definition	A company primarily owned by multiple family members that offers a product/service to the general public	The infrastructure that provides wealthy family members financial, tax, legal, accounting, philanthropic, and other concierge services
Primary purpose	Deliver a product/service into the market; provide competitive return for owners	Protect and grow family capital; serve the back office needs of family members
Often managed as	Moneymaker; maximize growth and profit	Cost center; take care of administrative functions
Family's role in management	Typically one or more family members in key chairman, CEO, and executive leadership roles	Older generations commonly maintain certain decision-making until the next generation is in their forties or later
Level of professionalism	Typically high, especially in larger and profitable, growing entities	Varies significantly; some are professionally run, and others are resource deprived
Governance	Ranges—for public companies, high; for privately held companies, often low	Ranges from zero to sophisticated governance systems, typically in G3+ family offices
Succession rates	High	Low

Finally, there's often a desire for subsequent generations to seek out roles in the family business, often leadership roles. That's not necessarily true of family offices; subsequent generations don't necessarily want to serve in the office at all, much less take charge of it. One reason is perhaps this: for many principals, the family office (perhaps in its current state) just isn't that interesting. Dealing with investments, accountants, and attorneys isn't engaging for many people. By contrast, if your family business is, say, creating an interesting product or producing interesting services via its operations, it's more likely to attract the interest of family members.

If you ask family office principals—the main recipients of its services—what the purpose of the family office is, most will report that it is to protect, manage, and grow family capital and to manage many of the related work streams—estate planning, accounting, taxes, philanthropy, and some concierge services such as travel. They see the family office's purpose—in essence—as about making money for the principals, whereas a family foundation and any philanthropic activity are about giving money away, for the broader society.

The offices that have broadened their purpose to include benefiting the broader society (while still taking care of the principals' needs; that is table stakes, after all) are much more engaging for the subsequent generations of family members to work in and, therefore, will prove to be more sustainable. The family office, in a sense, acts as a family business, an entity that provides services to the broader society, not just the family principals.

Depending on how the office is set up, the family members might serve as part of its leadership, as part of the office board, or on committees, or they might have a vote in who does participate in its governance. They might have a say in the direction of the office—and therefore of the wealth it manages. They might determine or be part of the office's succession plan—who will run the office in the future. Family office leadership allocates the family's financial assets such as liquid investments; makes decisions on allocations into alternative assets, including real estate and private equity; and sets governance for nonfinancial assets such as vacation properties and artwork.

All this is to say that family offices are a complex private structure that should be designed to meet the specific needs of the family. Though separate from the family business, the family office is indeed a business. To sustain your family's wealth—and the good that wealth can do for the family and the world—through multiple generations, the family office will support the family best when it is thoughtfully designed and managed like other professionally run companies.

Flexibility

Flexibility is also crucial for the sustainability of the family office. An anonymous successful manufacturing company in the US that remains privately held by the family has a corporate charter that actually prevents family members from serving in full-time roles. This stipulation is designed to attract professional nonfamily talent to the organization. The family, however, is active in the governance of the operating company and of the family office. In fact, the family office was set up by the fourth generation of the family as a vehicle to keep the family together and to provide a variety of services to help the family be the best owners of the business possible.

The vision for this family office was to explicitly respect the fact that the various family owners all had different needs and abilities, and they wanted to have a culture where they could show up as they are. If a member needed to take a time-out from family office roles and responsibilities for a few years to focus on their career or their own family, they could, and they could return to a more active role in the office later without repercussions. Their belief was that the more involved the family was in the office, the better they would be in the operating company as stewards.

Whereas prior generations of the family may have valued the collective more, the current generation saw the need to recognize the individual more and believed that doing so would enable a better outcome for the collective. If you wanted to lead a significant part of the family office—great—but do it with your best effort. If you wanted to be a passive shareholder, that was okay too.

Family meetings: be there, or be talked about.

A simple example is family meetings. Historically, each member was required to be there. "Be there, or be talked about" was the informal motto.

Yet the fourth generation realized that a binary mode of contributing was unwise. Playing a limited role was now permissible. The culture allowed it, and the family clarified what its shareholders are required to do and what privileges they receive. The same was true for more involved modes of participation. The important thing was that the culture allowed for various ways to engage.

With flexibility and a carefully designed family office, the family has managed to sustain their wealth and their stewardship in the family business. Without that willingness to change with the needs of each generation and perhaps each member, the younger family members could have disengaged or felt their needs weren't being met. The family office is not a monolith; it's a tool for financial sustainability that functions best when it reflects the sometimes-changing needs of its users.

One of the beautifully unique factors about a family office is that it has both a head and a heart. Both of these are necessary when you are making key decisions. Various family members may view decisions with one lens over the other. For example, vacation properties owned by the family members are often not terribly good investments of capital. Family vacation properties sometimes get only a handful of weeks of usage a year, and you can easily rent top-end houses all over the world, so renting often makes more financial sense. A financial analyst may recommend selling the family vacation property, saving the family money each year (the head). Yet the family vacation property may be a galvanizing factor in keeping the family together, creating opportunities for siblings and cousins to interact and build bonds (the heart). It may represent decades of important family memories for some members, including a connection to the older generations who are no longer present. The heart may say to keep the vacation property because it provides nonfinancial benefits for the family.

The head and the heart are collaborative; they need not be at the expense of each other. As with many things, defining where the office as a whole stands is the most important starting point. With clarity and transparency about who is involved and what the office does, you can avoid misunderstandings and confusion. Your own family office will be prepared to support the family for many generations to come.

WHAT WORKS

- Having open communication about how the family business and family office are similar and different in terms of management, governance, and family participation

WHAT DOESN'T

- Failing to proactively determine and communicate what role spouses or other family members outside the direct family lineage to G1 will have in the family office

CHAPTER 2

Preparing the Family

Books upon books are written on how to introduce children to wealth for the few families in this world who have this fortunate situation, and I am no expert. But from my perspective, my father got some things right. He was open about his business with the family. He shared the day's events with us, was always open to answering questions, and talked openly about people-related issues at work. He worked hard to integrate his family into the business: my siblings and I worked summer jobs at the family business, we attended the summer company picnic and local trade shows, and he encouraged us to join the business over the years. And he instilled a strong yet balanced work ethic, leading by example. He was often home by five p.m. and didn't work too much on the weekends. Could he have done some things a bit different, from my perspective? I believe the one thing he could have done better was to prepare me for the talk.

Because my father's company was successful financially, by the time of my coming of age in middle school and high school, the family benefited from the success of my father's hard work. We lived in a beautiful home in a lovely suburb. My father and mother enjoyed collecting art together, going on nice family vacations, and going to sporting events from time to time.

As a kid, this was all mostly a positive feature, but sometimes it was not. I was a bit shy growing up, so at times I did feel self-conscious about having a large house and about the family trips we'd take over the holidays. I never wanted to be known as the "rich kid," and I developed a terrible fear of people wanting to be friendly with me because of my money or because I had a fun house to play in. And while my father would be open with us kids about work issues, he rarely spoke to us about money—how much we had, how to care for it, and so on. I believe some of this was due to my father's own parents, who, as immigrants, likely were humble and relatively simple people. This may have instilled an underdog mentality in my father, who passed that framing on life to me in many ways.

When I hit twenty-one years of age, my father casually mentioned that I should set up a one-on-one meeting at Ted Chase's downtown office. All I knew of Ted was that he was my father's attorney. I had spoken with him only a few times. Maybe once or twice, as he was usually included in the management offsites in my family's kitchen.

At the time, I was a senior in college, and the idea of getting myself to the downtown financial district where their offices were located wasn't all that appealing, especially since I didn't know what the purpose of the meeting was. After trying my best delay tactics, I finally gave in to my father's request and set up a meeting with Ted.

I recall feeling a bit awkward walking into some random tall building in the city, entering into a professional office space with a bunch of cubicles, saying hello to the receptionist, and feeling like I was being treated like some VIP. "Can I get you some water?" "How is Northwestern going?" "Do you know what you might do for your summer work?"

I was led into a somewhat spacious window office, where Ted was behind a big wooden desk, many stacks of papers and briefs piled in front of him and on a credenza behind him. I think it may have been the first time I was ever in a business meeting. I felt uncomfortable.

I remember thinking that, compared to me, a youthful whipper-snapper, barely twenty-one years old, Ted seemed like an ancient oak. Basically, at my age then, anyone who was older than thirty might as well have been ninety. Ted must have actually been in his early seventies at that point, and he spoke quite slowly and deliberately, which added to the mystique.

After one or two pleasantries, Ted jumped in. "Scott, now that you have reached your twenty-first birthday, it's time we have a talk."

I thought, Shit, what did I do? Did he find out I used to bring our housekeeper to the grocery store so I could buy beer in high school? Or maybe this was a setup, and the feds were waiting for me to turn twenty-one so I could be tried as an adult for something serious? My active imagination was hard at work.

"The fact is, your father has been setting aside money for you, just as he has done for both of your siblings, and the result of that, Scott, is that you are a wealthy young man. In fact, you may not need to worry about money again in your life."

This revelation was quite confusing. On one hand, I understood that our family had money, more than many of my peers, sure, but the notion that I might never have to worry about money seemed abstract, and quite honestly, I didn't immediately assume this was a good thing.

After dropping the news to me, I don't think I listened to another thing Ted said at that meeting. As he was diving deep into the details of various trusts, explaining how some of the family business stock was already in my name, etc., etc., I was still trying to decipher what it meant to never have to worry about money. In fact, what he was saying made me instead worry about the whole situation!

According to my mother, I had always been a bit rebellious. I was always asking questions, challenging the way things were in a healthy way. I am most certain this drove my parents, teachers, summer counselors—you name it—pretty crazy (sorry, folks). So part of me wanted to understand what this concept meant, and part of me wanted to push back and evaluate for myself whether this Ted fella, however well intentioned, knew what the heck he was talking about. I suppose, in the moment, I kind of shook my head politely and confirmed that I understood, but deep down, I was thinking, Okay, interesting data point, Teddy. Let's see if I can confirm this down the road.

Perhaps odder than Ted notifying me of my status as a person with some personal wealth—which, I suppose, he had a legal obligation to do as the family attorney—was the fact that my dad stuck him with the task. In hindsight, there could have been a bit more dialogue about what having this wealth might mean to me, as someone about to graduate from college. My father could have, at any point in my upbringing, helped me bring it down to reality and make it practical.

On the other hand, had Ted said something to the effect of "and here is how you can withdraw any of the funds, at the snap of your fingers," that may have had adverse consequences. "Vegas, here we come, baby!" kind of thing.

In my mind, my father (and my mother as well) should have been the main ones delivering the news. At the very least, they should have been there with Ted. Some setting of context would have been useful, too: How much and when would I be able to access the money? What were the expectations, if not the laws, in terms of how it could be used? It would have been helpful if they had checked in after a week or a month: What questions did the talk bring up? They could have brought the family together for a check-in now that this information was available to all of us.

Back then, my focus was on studying and figuring out my professional life, so I more or less discounted Ted's revelation—even ignored it. I knew my father wanted me to consider joining the family business, which I knew was a fortunate possibility to have as an option, but I also knew I needed to find the best path for me. Even if that meant joining the business at some point, I thought I'd benefit from some outside work experience.

My social circles in college were mostly business-focused guys, and in those circles, even as a junior, I saw that the best if not coolest jobs for business-focused guys were in management consulting or investment banking. Although I wouldn't say that the salary was the only scorecard, people knew what you made at the blue chip firms compared to a small boutique consulting firm and assigned social value to that. I wanted to have a generous salary out of college; I can't say I was driven by the intrinsic happiness that a job might provide. And within those fields, there was a hierarchy, of course: McKinsey and Goldman Sachs being the best. My point is that my mind was focused on how I was going to find a career, earn my own money, and here was this old timer telling me I didn't have to work. My young adult mind simply couldn't reconcile those two points, so I let it go.

As I neared the end of my college days, I decided that I didn't have the desire to dig into what Ted had told me. My plan was to get a high-paying job and start my career. And while I had enjoyed working a few summers at the family business, I also saw it as one and the same as the family wealth: I wasn't sure how I felt about working in the business, so at least then, I knew I needed to strike out on my own.

Working for The Man

So that's what I did. My first job out of college was one I found myself. I didn't use any connections to get it, and it was in a field where no one knew anything about me, my background, or my family's wealth.

And it was great. I loved seeing the paycheck each month. It was a huge boost to my self-esteem and helped me build confidence. And from that first job, my manager took me under his wing and encouraged me to pursue an MBA—which was something that I thought of from time to time—and to push myself to apply to the top schools.

This first job was in management consulting. I was a junior analyst on various engagements and was often assigned to cull through financial statements to help the partners at my firm do their analysis. Through it, I learned how to read financial statements. And since our consultancy specialized in turnaround—fixing troubled business situations—there was often a heavy dose of drama along with our engagements. One of my first assignments was with a family–owned and operated auto parts distribution business, one of the largest in the metropolitan area. The company had been chugging along for several decades, with marquee clients such as Ford and GM, under the leadership of the founding CEO. Why was this a turnaround situation? Well, it was a good lesson in family business succession. The patriarch had passed away suddenly, with no true succession plan in place. His son was trying his darnedest to run the company. The problem was that the son—we can call him Brett—had no experience in running a business of this size. Brett had never worked anywhere other than the family business. Much to the dismay of the other leaders in the company, he had been promoted often without proving himself and never had formal training. Fewer than eighteen months after the father passed away, the business was losing cash, customers, and key employees.

I was roughly six months out of college and was attending a board meeting of this company when I witnessed Brett break down in tears as he introduced our firm—the turnaround specialists—and explained that we were there to help him avoid selling the company to its creditors and losing everything his father had built over the last thirty-plus years.

It was ironic that, in this job where I explicitly had a strategy to avoid, at least for now, entering the family business, I ended up working with a family business as one of our clients. The experience taught me a few lessons that are applicable to both family businesses and family offices.

Talent doesn't always run in the family. While most successful businesspeople like to believe that their children are all a chip off the ole block, it just ain't so. The next generation may not even be interested in working in the family business, yet many successors feel pressured to take the reins from their parents. Talent matters—don't assume that just because G1 was a financial wizard, or a creative genius, or a brilliant marketer, that G2 members are too. Know the requirements of the job, and know who has which skills. Often one sees family offices where the wealth creator is "running the show" with respect to investments, and one of the G2 children—usually those with little or no business acumen—is put in a sidecar role with the family foundation. Perhaps there is room for more nuance than this?

Talent doesn't always run in the family.

For any organization worth extending past the founder, succession planning is not only important but often needed earlier than expected. This is probably the largest risk to an organization. Whether it's a Fortune 500 company, a small business, a family business, or indeed a family office, the sudden loss of a CEO or key executive can lead to its downfall. Succession is critical: Do you have a plan? Is it current? Have outside, nonfamily professionals provided input? Have the key stakeholders agreed to it?

In my view, family members who have the option of working in a family business—and let's recognize what an incredible privilege that is—have a responsibility to get at least one job in a totally different industry, without any connections, and earn their stripes a bit. In some cases, it is helpful to also get formal business training, such as an MBA. What I experienced, and what I hear from other family office members, is that an external job adds tremendously to their self-esteem, and the increased value to the family business should they choose to enter one day is irreplaceable. Had Brett done this, maybe his family business would still be around. Sadly, it shut down. By the time our firm got hold of it, even the turnaround artists couldn't make it work. Family members will be best prepared if they get outside experience; that will make their involvement in the family business all the more valuable. This applies to the family office too; if you've never run a business, you're probably not ready (at least without a good amount of training and support) to run the family office.

Working for Dad

After my work in the consultancy, I had an opportunity to join the family business. To be fair, I had always had the opportunity to join the family business. My father had made it abundantly clear to me that he'd welcome me joining the company. Now, with hindsight I recognize that this is such an incredibly lucky situation to have been in. Yet I was always somewhat hesitant to give the option serious thought.

I was the youngest of three siblings. I have great memories of growing up in a busy household. As the youngest, I was always anxious to hang out with my older siblings—especially my brother, since I was closest to him in age—and their friends. I wanted to try new things at the same time they were trying them. In general, I always wanted to accelerate time in an effort to catch up with them and be with and like them.

We all generally got along well throughout the years. Both of my siblings went to college, but their paths differed quite a bit afterward. The eldest, my sister, lived outside of our home city in her twenties and into her thirties, didn't choose a business path, and then returned to our hometown to raise her family. My brother, the middle sibling, four years older than me, was clearly interested in business from early on. After a brief stint on the East Coast, he returned to our hometown to work in the family business.

He loved it and was already achieving success by the time I had a few years of nonfamily work experience under my belt.

I was eventually ready to transition out of the management consultancy and was already thinking quite seriously about obtaining an MBA. I had a window of time before I'd likely start a program, and when I discussed the possibility of joining the business with my father, I certainly had some concerns.

First, bless his heart, in an effort to continually send the message that he wanted me to join and that I'd have the opportunity to rise and co-run the company, he would say, "Imagine you and your brother as copresidents one day!" I think this had the opposite effect that my father intended. For me, I heard, "Hey, come to run the family business! You will rise to the top—no matter what." Again, what a huge privilege, but to me, I saw it as an undeserved gift. And, darn it, I had worked hard in college and subsequently found a challenging job all by myself after college; I could do things on my own, Dad!

But here was an opportunity to make my father happy, which I think was the real driver of my decision. I didn't take the family job as a logical part of my career path, but I am very glad I did the stint. I had the chance to work on some fascinating parts of the business, help start a new product line, and see what it would be like to work in the family business. It helped dispel some myths I had believed. For example, I assumed I would not find the business an inherently interesting place to work. I also thought that I might be treated like the boss's son; I knew I'd resent that special treatment. I also imagined that I would clash with my sibling in the company. None of these proved to be accurate—yet these are common fears that many family members have with respect to working in the family business.

In the same way that I—as well as many experts in family business—believe that working outside of the family business is a must-have experience, so too was working inside the business. I would have greatly regretted it had I chosen to never work in the business, just to prove to myself and others that I could do things on my own. I would have been robbing myself of the chance to see if I really wanted it, and it would have potentially sent the wrong message to both my father, the CEO at the time, and my brother, who was rising nicely through the organization, that I didn't see the value in even trying it for a short stint.

Our First Family Office

Around this time, our first version of the family office came into existence. As is often the case with larger family-owned businesses, the staff from the family business were initially given additional responsibilities to support the family. The office was de facto run by Ted, who wore multiple hats: my father's personal attorney, the family business attorney, and the head of the family office embedded in the family business.

I shudder to think about the financial decisions he made on behalf of the family. As much as he was a highly competent attorney, as I understood it, his office had little investing expertise beyond managing the capital that our family business was throwing off. My father was hesitant if not downright skeptical of working with a professional money manager; in many instances, he valued familiarity and longevity over competence in terms of working with a specific provider. I think the entire strategy for managing the family liquid finances was something like this: put some in stocks; put some in bonds. Literally, that was it.

A few of the family business accountants were also gradually involved to support the family finances. One thing Ted did early on, to his credit, was pass on some of the shares of the family business to the G2 siblings. This was a game changer with respect to G2's future wealth; the value of these shares rose dramatically over the years and did so already in our respective estates. It is typically a good practice to push highly appreciating assets down to the next generation as early as possible. There were both control shares, held mostly by my father, and ownership shares, which were split among the G2 siblings. Still, at this point all the G2 members were over twenty-one years of age, but we were in the dark about what assets we owned and how those were being invested. This situation is likely due to my father's conservative outlook. Perhaps he was in some ways in denial about the wealth he was creating.

I could imagine him thinking at the time, What's the point of telling the kids about the money? They are young, and if anything, it may have a negative effect on their motivation. Besides, while the money may be here today, who knows about the future? Since they don't need it, they don't need to know about it.

Multiple conversations with wealth managers and estate planners have pointed to this philosophy as a common practice, especially for my father's generation. He was born during the Great Depression, after all.

The Road Less Traveled

It was now around 1995. I was a few years out of undergrad, and I was dead set on going to business school for an MBA. I didn't have a clear idea where my career path would take me after that, but I liked the idea of working in business and of being a professional at it, having a degree.

Unfortunately, my father didn't like this idea. In retrospect, he likely realized that if I went to business school, I might be lured into a sexier industry than what the family business was in, and ultimately, that is kind of how it played out. However, I wish he had been more supportive of me seeking a degree. Had he been, perhaps there would have been a better chance of me returning to the family business after school. Instead, in his eyes, I was crossing a line by venturing off to B-school, especially a snooty Ivy League one at that, and his disapproval added tension to our relationship at times.

Business school did indeed open my eyes. I rubbed shoulders with an incredible number of type A professionals, all with impressive academic and professional backgrounds, and all of whom seemed to have ambition levels a few notches above mine. The professors were inspiring, if not downright intimidating. Socially, the amount of partying—drinking in particular but sometimes more—was also a surprise. For the first six months, I could hardly keep up. It is also where I first was introduced to levels of wealth and prestige that I had never seen. Daughters of Global 1000 CEOs, sons of US senators, nephews of former presidents, cousins in multigeneration family offices—you had it all.

Although I never again worked in the family business, I certainly worked more and more with the family office, and I know my MBA taught me many important concepts that help me to this day with family office work.

First, I learned the power of the network. Using your professional network for introductions to key service providers is crucial for both personal and professional matters.

On a practical level, I learned how to evaluate a company. MBA programs expose students to a wide variety of industries over a short amount of time and teach ways to evaluate and analyze those industries. This is important for family office principals, who need to participate—even if only to oversee—with investment managers and asset allocators. Understanding a variety of industries is also helpful when it comes time to make a change in your own company, recognizing patterns of growth and decline that all fields undergo.

And most critically, I learned the self-confidence to dream big and learned that I could do it, whatever it may be. After I was accepted to business school but before committing to enroll, I recall having a conversation with a current faculty member and asking why I should choose Harvard over the other schools I was admitted to. His answer was both smug and to the point: "Because you will be able to look yourself in the mirror and know you can compete at the highest level in business." To be sure, I did find the environment quite arrogant on many occasions. Yet I believe the point is accurate. And I know I gained a sense of self-confidence from being anonymous (not the boss's son), being among many high performers, and being pushed to a pace that I never would have imagined otherwise.

Had I chosen to go into the family business, I believe I would have made an even larger impact by virtue of having the MBA. In my conversations with other family business owners and offices, taking time for an MBA is often a good trade-off for the experience you'd gain by working those two years in the company.

Unsuccessful Attempts at Integration

I got out of B-school in 1997, and the internet was just taking off. I started to get really excited about a career in tech. It was clear to me that the field would be an interesting place to work and would have many entrepreneurial opportunities.

I followed some of the best advice from a B-school professor about my first job out of school, and I give it out as much as possible to young graduates: "Pick an industry you find compelling, and get a job at the best company in that field." I pursued a job at Microsoft and secured an offer to join their brand-new division focused on internet businesses. It was like my MBA, in some ways: a competitive and driven culture, with a work-hard, play-hard ethos. Again, I enjoyed being anonymous and making my own bones.

Even though my father probably knew it was coming, it was difficult to explain to him after my MBA that I was joining Microsoft and moving to Seattle. He made it clear that he thought Bill Gates was a nerd, that the tech industry wasn't a well-respected field, and that Microsoft was an anticompetitive bully of a company. Rather than defending my career choice and hoping he might feel proud that I had joined a highly successful company, I had to bite my tongue and not say anything on several occasions. Again, this all added some strain to our relationship, and if anything, it backfired in terms of any desire I may have had to work in the family business. I don't hold any ill will on this. While we had different visions for my optimal career path, I do believe he always had my best interests in mind.

If you are trying to encourage the next generation to join your family business or even the family office, strong-arming or criticizing their choices is unlikely to convince them. You may just run them off. Instead, let them live their own lives. Encourage them to get experience and to learn about their future path, whether that's in your own company or not. If you love them, set them free. If they do decide to join you, that experience will be invaluable.

One place where I did participate with my father and siblings was in attending some family business seminars. Northwestern University was, at the time, a leader in family business research and teaching, led by an academic practitioner named John Ward. He'd produce these engaging family office summits every few years. My siblings and my father and I would join them, hoping to glean from other family businesses—many much larger than ours—some of the best practices in family management and succession.

Some of the takeaways from these seminars are crucial for leading family businesses, and I believe they apply to family offices as well. First, succession is both critical and yet often undervalued; it often hits you when you least expect it. Independent board members are critical and correlate with high-performing family businesses. Fair is not always equal; for example, it may be the fair thing to distribute voting shares of a family business only to those family members who are active in the business, even if the distribution of shares is not equal across the members. Money does not equal love; successors in a family are incorrect to assume that more money given to them equates to more love from the giver. There are times when giving less than is possible is the right thing to do. Finally, family is not always equal to management and should not always have equal ownership. This was displayed in terms of three partially overlapping circles—one for family members, one for management of the business, and one for ownership of the business. This is a terrific framework that applies to family offices in a similar fashion.

From one of the family business summits, we heard about a larger family business that had some family members involved in the legacy core business and others involved in a venture arm that the business had set up. This arm was responsible for finding interesting and synergistic businesses to invest capital into. This really piqued my interest; I was already interested in entrepreneurial ventures, and I saw this as a potential way to be involved in the family business in a manner that I found compelling, and where I might chart my own course. I asked my father about what this company had done and whether he could ever see something similar happening at our family business. I think the question caught him off guard; on one hand, he very much wanted me to enter the company, but I think he also had a singular vision of how that would look if I were to do it. Perhaps he simply didn't believe that the company needed to have such a new function.

It is also possible that I could have participated in an investment role within the family office, had I known that such capital existed. This is something to think about for parents who may have a set vision of how their children should work in the family business, and who also may discount a successor's ability to work in the family office. It's good general parenting advice, too: Your children will have their own vision of their future. You can try to push them into yours, but it rarely works—and when it does, it can lead to resentment. Instead, help them develop who they want to be—not who you want them to be. In the end, their genuine intrinsic interest and commitment will mean better outcomes for the family business, the family office, and even the family itself.

Paper Rich, Cash Poor

"Cash is king" is a phrase often used in entrepreneurial circles. It is a reminder that no matter how well things may look for a company—marquee clients, credentialed executives, high-profile venture backers, and so on—if there is not sufficient free cash flow to fund the business, at some point, it can threaten the very existence of the company. The same concept applies to people, too. In my family, fortunately, no one has been ruined financially. Yet it is an important topic that exists at different levels, in most families. I share it in the hope it might help other families deal with or even prevent these types of disasters.

In wealthy families, there is the perception that the family members have way too much wealth and that they don't even know what to do with it all. Certainly, that is true in certain situations. But there are also many family members in wealthy families who do utilize all of their capital, and there are even those who end up consuming all of their capital and end up with nothing or far less than they need later in life.

Unfortunately, I've known people in this last category. One individual—let's call her Alice—is part of a very wealthy family. She received a large amount of funds along with other family members earlier in her life yet is now in a position where her liquid assets are almost out. This has put unnecessary stress on the rest of their family, who will have to serve as the backstop. Alice was a competent person in all dimensions of her life. She had a professional degree and at one point worked as a professional in a large firm. Yet later in life, through a variety of circumstances, she found herself in financial straits. The stereotype of wealthy inheritors who haven't a clue about money, budgets, or accountability is often true; those types exist. Some are wealthy enough they can skate over any financial stress. Others have families that will always bail them out, no questions asked. Others land in trouble and have no backstop.

From where I sit, part of the problem was that Alice felt somewhat entitled to not only the money she received but also to ongoing support from her closest relatives. Over the years, her family tried to help her with wealth and budgeting, but she didn't see the very real threat of running out of money. She felt there were no consequences for her unlimited spending.

A huge part of the problem was a lack of accountability. Alice was making all her financial decisions without consulting her family members or unpaid advisors; all the while her paid advisors kept other family members in the dark—perhaps in part due to the high fees they were taking from Alice. Soon after coming into this wealth—which came as a lump sum—Alice went on a spending spree and started a business that lost money for many years in a row.

Privacy is another reason. Alice often didn't care to discuss her financial matters with the family. She felt a bit ashamed about it and perhaps also thought that it wasn't their business. At various points throughout the years, she explicitly instructed her financial advisors not to share details about her wealth management with the family.

The quality of the advisors was yet another issue. The financial advisors were not doing a good job on her behalf, which helped her justify not sharing with the rest of her family. At one point late in the relationship with a prominent local financial management firm, it became apparent that Alice's registered investment advisor (RIA) fees were 125 basis points, when they should have been around 75 or below. The family members, through some resistance, convinced Alice to work with another manager who was charging appropriately. This move alone saved Alice a significant amount of money each year.

The way most financial advisors charge is based on assets under management (AUM), and they set a percentage such as 0.5 percent or 1.0 percent. Each 1 percent represents 100 basis points, so if an advisor charges 1 percent, that is 100 basis points, or bps. At first glance, the difference between 50 and 100 basis points may seem inconsequential, but in the family office world, paying 50 bps more than typical could translate into millions of dollars in unnecessary fees. And in Alice's case, this had been happening for well over twenty years, costing her a huge sum.

The point of this story is that anyone—no matter how rich they may be at one point—can undo their situation without planning, accountability, and support. It happens all the time. Many factors eat away at wealth—professional fees, taxes, expenses, inflation. As challenging as it is to create substantial wealth, in many cases, it is even harder to maintain it over the years. Had Alice been better prepared for her windfall, she might have approached its management differently.

You can help set your own children up for a better outcome by having the talk early and encouraging financial literacy. Education is crucial—finance, business, and so on—although it doesn't have to be formal education. Support from the other principals or G1 is crucial, as is an unbiased perspective—truthful advice from a trustworthy source, like a neutral advisory committee composed of people who don't make money off the principal. But the family office can also play a role in supporting people like Alice. It can provide a buffer between her and her family members so she doesn't feel ashamed of her situation. It can also provide accountability and can advise her toward a more sustainable use of her funds.

Good Stewards

There are many ways to set your family up for success in their lives after an inheritance. Creating good stewards of the family fortune is the same as creating good people: you provide transparency and support, encourage them to seek out life and work experience, and offer guidance when they are willing to hear it.

Education is one crucial component of financial responsibility. This doesn't mean that every member of G2 needs to have an MBA, but it does mean that their particular financial situation requires a certain level of financial literacy. I am working on a sort of financial and investing training curriculum for my kids. Having heard from other family offices that they have had success bringing this education to kids at an early age, I am inspired to start early. I used to think twenty-one years of age was the right time to begin this education, but if the person already has free access to their wealth, the knowledge may come too late.

Perhaps even more important than teaching facts is accountability. We all need to know how to be responsible with money; open discussions and structure help create that. My wife and I are also working on ways to establish budgets for our daughters to help teach the value of money, the value of hard work. This year and last summer, our older daughter worked and earned some real spending money; most of her friends are not yet doing so. I have seen how she feels a sense of pride for what she has earned, and I trust that she will be prepared when the time comes for her to join the family office in some capacity.

Support and guardrails are also crucial. When someone makes a mistake, such as running an unprofitable business for more years than it needs to, having a familial support system can save them from flushing good money after bad. It can also help to structure the way their money is released to them; a lump sum can become too much to manage too quickly. With estate planning and the next generation, it is customary to have phased releases at various set milestones (e.g., when the person reaches twenty-five, then thirty-five, then forty-five years of age). In Alice's case, phasing out the release of assets could have helped her sustain her personal wealth longer—or indefinitely.

Finally, business expertise can provide more knowledge to make better decisions. When concepts like gross margin and net profit are not theoretical but lived experiences, you begin to understand how money works and how it can work for you. Every family member should work in an operating business, even if only for a year or two, if they are to bring value to whatever their role is in the family office.

WHAT WORKS

- G1 supporting and even encouraging G2 to work in the family business and to embrace other educational experiences of the business

- The checks and balances of family members looking after each other

WHAT DOESN'T

- Introducing inheritors to their capital via a third party and not family, and any similar lack of transparent communication about how to best manage the capital

- Providing family members access to a substantial amount of capital without providing baseline education on financial planning and budgeting

CHAPTER 3

Purpose, Vision, and Values

What will your family office do, and how do you want to get there? Purpose, vision, and values will answer those questions for you. They are core components of any business, and the family office is no exception. In my experience, only a minority of offices have done the work to think through these important topics and codify them, yet those who have swear by the benefit of the activity.

The family office's purpose tells you why it exists. The purpose clarifies who it serves. And it includes what services it offers. Before you can begin building your family office, I've found it crucial to envision what you want it to be. How will you measure success? Your values underlie how you want to operate your structure. What principles do you want it to adhere to?

Clearly identifying your purpose, vision, and values will set your family office up for success. These elements can help you answer questions and make good choices, with the future of your family office always at the center. The very process of defining these important topics, when done collaboratively with other family principals, has an important trust and community-building element across the family.

Purpose

A clear and compelling purpose enables the office to prioritize. It fosters proper resource deployment and engages the whole family. Think about building a home. You might articulate that the home's purpose is to provide a comfortable living space, with plenty of fun features for entertaining, and ample outdoor land with inspiring views. It is intended for the core family, including two parents and three kids, two pets, and a part-time residence for in-laws. You can see how this purpose is specific but also directed for one family's particular needs; you might not have pets or need space for your in-laws, so your home would be different. The same is true for the family office: an effective purpose reflects the unique needs of your family, and it may also leverage unique strengths that your family possesses.

Indeed, a baseline of a family office is to invest capital, file taxes, distribute funds, and the like. These are the minimum requirements, necessary but not sufficient if one wants to create a sustainable family office that engages generations of principals and achieves its potential. We will take it for granted that any family office has the baseline purpose of investing, tax management, and so on, but that is just a starting point. It's like saying you want to build a house, and you want it to keep the rain out and have running water—yes, of course you do.

You might ask, though, What if you don't have a purpose? Do you really need one? According to Peter Moustakerski, CEO of the Family Office Exchange (aka FOX), this is one of the classic mistakes that family office principals make: not creating a shared purpose. If you have inherited a family office, you will need to refresh it to ensure that, rather than relying on the elder generation's purpose, the current generation is bought into it. As a family office grows and you move from siblings to cousins, the variety of points of view and experiences necessitates proper planning to identify and operationalize a shared purpose.

As Peter puts it, the family office principals need to ensure that the family office is driven by demand, not constrained by supply.

The family members—the human beings the office represents—must be front and center. If the structure is misaligned with those people's needs, it will fail. You might not expect this for an organization whose focus is financial planning and support, but human capital is more important than financial capital. James Hughes, who has written several wonderful books on family offices, makes this important point over and over.

> The family office principals need to ensure the family office is driven by demand, not constrained by supply.

How do you define your family office purpose?

In order to ensure buy-in from the other principals, defining your family office purpose must be a collaborative process. What matters to each person? The best purposes have some connection to the outside world, a way to make a difference. A purpose will inspire additional principals to be involved and to want the endeavor to succeed. The purpose is something the family cares about and has some expertise in. A family whose wealth comes from real estate may want a component of its mission to support affordable housing, for example. The family office purpose doesn't have to be purely philanthropic, but it is most effective when it is compelling to the principals, collaborative among all of the principals, and valuable to each of them as well.

When I got to the point that I was setting up a new family office specifically for my family line, I already had an operating company that was distinct from the family office, and I determined that my operating company and the newly formed family office would both benefit from a tight alignment. The purpose of my family office became to enable the purpose of the operating company.

This has resulted in the creation of a few entities under the ONE WORLD moniker. There are both family office entities (for the benefit of the family) and family businesses (to provide outside services to those outside of the family). ONE WORLD's mission is to enable organizations to scale social impact and to improve the lives of individuals globally. The broad nature of this purpose allows us to approach it from many possible directions.

The mission statement can help make your purpose concrete. For example, a mission statement such as "to support our descendants to pursue their passions and reach their potential" helps provide focus for the office. The ONE WORLD mission statement is more externally focused; this other example above is internally focused, but what matters is that there is a focus. Both approaches are suitable; there's no judgment here!

As a result of aligning my operating company and my family office, the business is stronger due to the capital it can access, and the office is stronger with my direct supervision and involvement. I was able to focus on the family office rather than treating it as evening and weekend work. This is a good lesson, so I'll repeat it: treat the office with the same level of professionalism as other operating businesses—in terms of the time spent, the attention paid, resources invested, professionals hired, and so on.

Your family office can create a powerful tool for doing good in the world: for every dollar that a wealthy family gives to philanthropy, they typically have many multiples more in the office that could be put to use. I realized I had access to capital that could be put into projects aligned with my operating company. I first created the ONE WORLD fund so I could allocate money through the family office without having to fundraise externally. Instead of having an RIA build a portfolio of somewhat random assets I had no connection to, I could direct the office's investments to align with ONE WORLD's mission. With this purpose established, I had a line of sight to what protecting and growing wealth would lead to: more capital for my operating companies to achieve their mission.

Figure 3.1. Family/Family Office/Family Business

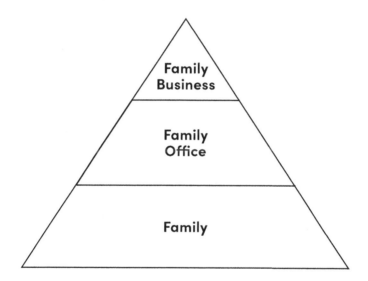

The interplay between three important elements—family members, the family office, and the family business—can be visualized as a pyramid, like that in figure 3.1. The family office faces inward, with its purpose to serve family, connecting it with the family business—an existing operating company, if one is in existence, or one that can be created to further the mission of the office and family. Having an external orientation and set of activities is how a pure family office can broaden and carry out its purpose beyond an office that may have a purpose and a suite of activities concerned solely with making money for the family.

This same external purpose can be fulfilled in other ways. If you do not have an operating company to support your purpose, an obvious place to look may be the family foundation, if you have one. You can also think about the causes the family cares deeply about, which may be evident in your philanthropic giving to date and the list of organizations members of the family volunteer for. A family foundation has a purpose identified in its charter, and your family office can align resources to support that purpose. Each of these options gets your family office closer to the purpose of serving the world in whatever way you or your family deems important. Your family office's specific purpose may evolve over time and may diverge from your other entities; that's fine. The office's purpose guides how it supports the family, whatever that support may need to be.

Who gets to define purpose?

Along the way, you'll need to determine who makes this sort of decision. Every family member may want a say, or some of them may leave it in your hands—or those of whoever is running the office.

In my case, I was flying solo. My brother and I each decided to start our own family offices; my sister decided to procure family office services from outside vendors. When I branched off on my own, I had free rein to create the office however I needed. This is a huge advantage but also daunting. My wife was working through health issues. My daughters were too young to provide meaningful input, still in grade school. So, although my immediate family couldn't yet contribute to the decision-making process, I set up the family office for my family line to serve me, my spouse, and my kids. One day (if the wealth hasn't been dissipated), it is certainly possible that my children will choose to leave my family office and start their own, but my aim is to create an office that will be flexible to adjust to their needs and allow them to put their fingerprints on it when they come of age, rather than see the entity as the older generation's, too set in its ways to meet their needs. But when the office represents a broader number of individuals who are at the age and stage they can participate, it becomes a fabulous opportunity to engage the family on this topic.

The questions that warrant consideration include who the office needs to serve. Beyond the principals, who are the other stakeholders? They might include the principals' spouses, if those spouses are not defined as principals. As mentioned, the principals are often limited to the bloodline; stakeholders are the tangential beneficiaries, who typically hold less decision-making power. This is the family definition again. Other stakeholders may include in-laws (again, if they are not officially principals), nonfamily members who work in the family office, and the vendors who provide services to the family office. You'll need to think deeply about what services the office should provide, beyond the traditional family office services of wealth management.

Vision

Once the key decisions for purpose are set, then you may move on to establish a vision for your family office. This can be thought of as an architect's blueprint, like a high-level floor plan. In getting to this step, to be well informed, you will be most prepared if you have visited at least four or five family offices of a similar size (in both number of generations/principals served and assets under management) to help you determine what you need and what your preferences are. This is a form of benchmarking, of ensuring that you're seeing all the possibilities of what a family office can do and how it may be structured.

In our family we did some of this, but it was too thin a pass to glean a whole lot. It is important to really dig in: What are the roles of the principals, the size and type of staff, the challenges in managing the family office? What has worked well, and what has not? These visits are ideally in person; a human connection can do wonders for helping your contact open up. An in-person meeting also lets you see their vision in context. An email might mean you get a slide deck, but your contact may lay out a detailed vision for their office if you are face-to-face and get into some of the human dynamics, which is always valuable. Take what you can get, of course, but networking helps here. Often, family principals are proud of what they have built and are eager to share with other family office principals; they may also be interested in your feedback. Approach this process with an open mind, and be sure to ask why certain features were built and which ones were perhaps deliberately left out.

What types of entities do you need, and how many of each? For example, LLCs are good legal entities to hold assets. A C corporation could be the overall management company of the family office. Trusts are a distinct legal entity that have a role in all family offices. At this stage you may think critically not only about the mechanical questions such as "Who will form my trusts, LLCs, and other entities?" but also about the higher-level questions like "What is the purpose of such entities?" and "What is the family trying to achieve with them?" Does the family envision that the office will have an internally created private equity function or will include innovative philanthropic activities or will manage family vacation properties? If so, the office needs the proper resourcing of people and budget to do so. Purpose informs vision in terms of scope, which informs structure down the road.

Again, this is a collaborative process: How does your vision compare to that of other family members who will operate under the same office? The structure you choose will operate most smoothly if it meets the needs of everyone included in the office. You can start with an existing template if that seems less daunting: Of the other family offices you have studied, which of them best represents what you are trying to build? You can benchmark that office to learn the pros and cons of their approach.

What will your role be in this structure? What are you good at that might benefit the office? What are you not good at, which you'll want someone else to do?

Your family office's vision is the purpose in context. If you have principals of age, you will want to bring them into the process, to tag along while you visit those other family offices. Once you put your insights on paper, envision your own office as clearly as possible.

This is where benchmarking again is useful. I needed to see several different types of family office structures to determine what I liked and what made sense for me.

It's crucial for the family office principals to create their own vision for the office that is not overly influenced by outside professionals. Yes, you will benefit from looking at what others have done to get inspiration, but the vision must be unique to your situation; no outside person should decide that for you. Family office principals are best served by understanding their needs and coming up with a vision independently of what an advisor or provider may suggest. The opportunity for a conflict of interest is simply too great, however professional and well intentioned the provider may be. But this self-directed vision will also be much closer to its final form because of your personal involvement. No outsider can ever know your family's needs as well as you do, and you will learn even more about them as you go through this process.

Values

There are no right or wrong values, just articulated and unarticulated ones. Before you begin the hands-on work of building your family office, you will benefit from having a set of values that it will adhere to. These work best if they are specific to you and the principals of your family office.

The values you identify for your family office might include investing for the maximum return. You might want to always ensure that the family comes first. You might even include criteria for a family member's involvement or leadership of the office. Whatever values you end up with will guide the family office forward. Your decisions, your structure, and even your use of the office must align with these values.

For ONE WORLD, they are:

- A long-term, total-impact perspective

- Innovation and experimentation

- Privacy for family with figures, yet public with practices

One crucial value for **every** principal: respect the challenge at hand in building and managing a family office. It is a complex company—often a collection of complex companies—and it needs to have the proper energy, capital, and time invested to make the company run successfully. Many individuals don't seem to fully grasp that they are starting an entirely new company and underestimate the task at hand. As has been said many times, making money and preserving money are generally two very different things, requiring different skills. At the same time, the family office founder or newly appointed successor doesn't want to appear unwise or unable to accept the challenges of this new leadership position and, as such, may let their ego get in the way and not raise their hand for help when it is needed.

> There are no right or wrong values, just articulated and unarticulated ones.

Your purpose gives your family office a meaningful reason to exist. Your vision gives you a map for putting that purpose into practice. And your values drive how you'll make decisions to support your purpose along the way. With all three pieces in place, you know why and how your family office will function; now you can focus on the mechanics of the office itself.

WHAT WORKS

- Establishing your family office with an overarching purpose in mind, a clear vision, and a clear set of values, with other stakeholders

WHAT DOESN'T

- Insufficient benchmarking with other family offices to learn how their purpose and operations were formed and how they are revised over time

CHAPTER 4

The Right Structure

Twenty-twenty was an exceptionally challenging year for the planet, and so it was for our family as well. The first few months of the year, the family was just starting to contemplate alternate structures for the family office, and each family member was beginning to think about their needs. And then COVID hit.

In mid-March of that year, things started to change dramatically. Travel, events, and work environments all changed and went into lockdown. No one knew what was happening, how long it would last, or the implications it would have down the line. Around this time, I decided I wanted to move my liquid investments from the existing family office I had with my father and siblings to a new registered investment advisor, one that could fully support my desire to invest sustainably and to have more control of my capital but still remain in the existing family office. One of my siblings soon also decided to move their family line capital to a new provider. These changes involved a lot of moving parts and occurred over several months.

While this transition was underway in the fall of 2020, one of our family members got into a serious car accident, which could have easily been fatal. It shook all of us to our core—as did my father's passing just a month later and the family office manager's resignation soon after. These events caused me to think about the real possibility of my mortality in a much more tangible way than ever before and also to give thought to the family office—and its sustainability—in a whole new way. I could no longer assume that concepts like succession planning and next-generation engagement were decades or even years away. It became very obvious that tragedy strikes anyone and everyone—and never when you expect or plan for it. Had I been on the receiving end of a fatal blow, all the momentum of the family office to date, as well as all my hopes and dreams for what it could turn into, would come to a screeching halt. I was positioned to leave my family a whole bunch of complex legal entities, undefined work processes, and complexity that would take them quite a bit to figure out without the proper planning and documentation.

My family was still mourning my father's passing, my close relative was doing slightly better after his near-death car crash, the pandemic was raging, and our family office situation was unstable due to the former manager's unexpected departure. If I ever needed a burning platform to provide an incentive to build my own family office, I now had it staring me in the face.

While a family office structure made sense for our family, it is not universally the right call. Even in situations when a person or family might suddenly have a great deal of liquidity—think the sale of a closely held business—it's wise to evaluate whether it makes sense to create a family office structure for yourself and when to do so.

Frank Ghali is the CEO of Jordan Park, a multifamily office registered investment advisor (RIA) based in San Francisco that works with many first-generation wealth creators, including a number of technology founders who have come into a material amount of prosperity very rapidly. According to Frank, "In these types of situations, I recommend that the wealth owner become knowledgeable about their options—and the costs in time and money of hiring a team internally. Indeed, the first steps are working with a well-regarded estate attorney, a CPA, and an RIA who is a fiduciary." This trio of specialists is a good jumping-off place to determine if you need (and want) to have more of a complete office.

Family Office Structure Options

There are three basic options for structuring the family office: If your family has a family business, the office can be embedded into your family business; this tends to work best when your needs from the office are relatively simple and uniform across the people the office serves. A multifamily office (MFO) is another option; this would be a professional firm that either specializes in family office work or performs these services alongside other financial services. These professionals can handle more complex needs than a family-business-attached office, but their attention may be spread among many clients, and, as Frank mentioned above, their intentions may not always align with yours. Finally, when your needs can no longer be met by the two previous options, you may need to set up a dedicated single family office (SFO). You may hire outside professionals to manage this SFO, or you or another of the principals may decide to run the office yourself. This, again, comes down to your specific needs and whether you believe an outsider—however professional and experienced they may be—can meet the needs and budget and time you and other principals have to invest. No matter what, it is absolutely key to have a skilled and motivated member of the family highly involved, especially in the early days.

Embedded in the Business

Version 1.0 of our family office was as an add-on to the family business—the embedded family office. While this model is fairly common, especially in the early days of the initial family office, it is also risk prone if you don't take into account a true separation of staff, resources, and accounting. In our case, the main functions it provided were estate planning, accounting, taxes, and investment management.

Some aspects of this situation worked quite well. G1 (my father) was familiar with the family business staff, having worked with them in some cases for decades. My father intimately trusted these folks, and I think for him that mattered more than anything. He could direct his attention to growing the family business and not worry about how the capital was managed.

Other aspects did not work so well. Our needs were becoming more complicated, and the office was getting to a point that it required a dedicated professional who had the right expertise and who would have brought in another professional to manage the liquid investments either in-house or via an RIA relationship. As adults, the members of G2 should also have had some visibility into their personal balance sheet, which we did not have in the embedded version of the office. Many families delay the communication of family wealth until the next generation is into their forties or even later. This can prevent the principals from fully understanding the options they have available, and it may cause them to pass up potential career paths—whether in the family business, the family office, or a third-party organization.

Moving to a Multifamily Office

We had the family office embedded within the business for roughly a decade, and it seemed to work just fine for our needs at the time. G2 (my siblings and I) were pretty oblivious of the activities, but we saw our investment portfolios growing. Leave well enough alone was the sentiment, but that can only be effective for so long.

However, around 2010, our family began to realize it was outgrowing the structure. One of the individuals we worked with at the law firm, who was managing the estate planning for the family, mentioned that he was considering moving to an RIA that managed investments for a few large families in our metropolitan area. Feeling that our needs might be better served, we decided to move our investment activity with him to this new firm and also to promote him to managing more of the family office activities—coordinating with the tax, legal, estate, and accounting professionals.

A multifamily office (MFO) is typically a third-party, separately owned entity from the family. It serves multiple families with no connection to each other. Some MFOs focus on financial services; others branch into additional services.

There were pros and cons with this setup. Because this individual's firm served several clients, not just our family, we didn't receive great service and, at times, the turnaround times for our requests were slow. Yet, I don't think the family had any point of comparison. While we had done occasional benchmarking with respect to family businesses, we only did a little bit of benchmarking with other family offices. We didn't give much consideration to whether our family office matters were complex enough to warrant a dedicated family office.

On the plus side, we benefited from the expertise of professionals working on multiple client matters, and our cost structure was shared among those other clients of the firm where our funds were managed.

An individual or a single family unit may be able to manage their affairs just fine without creating an in-house office. Our family maintained this structure and worked with the nonfamily member in the role of family office manager for approximately five years, generally without major issues or too much exposure to alternate models of family offices.

Moving to a Single Family Office

In situations where there may be a need for a high degree of customization (for example, going deep in one asset class), with multiple family members across multiple generations, or with a high variety of asset types, a single family office structure will serve the needs best.

Single family offices, which come in infinite varieties, are defined by one or more legal structures that serve the family members directly. Some are for a single family line; others work with multiple branches or family units. And if an SFO subsequently decides to manage capital for nonfamily members, which brings on a whole set of complexities and legal requirements, it effectively becomes an MFO.

Table 4.1. Family Office Comparisons: Embedded, MFO, and SFO

OFFICE STYLE	EMBEDDED	MFO	SFO
Definition	An office within the family business	A company that serves multiple, unrelated families	A private structure that serves one family (may be single family line or multiple family lines)
Purpose	Serve the financial and other back office needs of the family while relying on the human and financial capital of the family business	Serve the financial and other back office needs of multiple clients (families, individuals, foundations, and other entities)	Serve the financial and other back office needs of one family
Business model	Functions as part of the family business, using staff and resources to manage the family's financial assets	MFOs may earn fees based on the assets under management, consulting, or some other arrangement	Typically a cost center, the SFO can charge family members pro rata for services to cover costs

Level of customization	Low	Medium	High
Cost	Low	Medium	High
Time and effort for principal	Low	Medium	High
Generally best for	Small families (i.e., two generations or fewer); Simple structures; Few family members or few divergent needs	Smaller families; Simple structures; Family members who don't want or have expertise to manage professionals in-house	Larger, multigenerational families; Complex structures; Family members who bring strong business management expertise
Advantages	No need to hire a firm or team; Lowest cost of the three options	Clients benefit from service providers who work on multiple diverse clients and bring a variety of experiences and perspectives; Lower cost than SFO; Company does not have to manage staff; easier to move to new providers	Dedicated team likely to provide better service levels than MFO
Disadvantages	The staff likely has low/no experience managing family assets; the team will have other priorities—running the business—and limited time for the family office	Undedicated team not as customized; May be less inclined to do one-off projects	Cost is highest; Family has to manage staff; providers may have limited outside perspective

It was now roughly 2015, and during one of the quarterly check-ins with the family office manager, he mentioned that the RIA he was part of wasn't meeting his needs or the family's. He said it would be a good idea to bring things internal and create our own SFO. The idea of going internal seemed worth pursuing, and the family asked him to do some research and report back. Some weeks passed, and eventually the manager did report back with a plan of how he was going to create a custom SFO for our family. As a family that was becoming increasingly accustomed to personalized service, we liked the sound of customization. Here was an opportunity to hire him internally and to have him create something 100 percent bespoke for the family. Additionally, the manager said that we'd be able to create a family bank of sorts—to allow members to borrow against a family entity instead of a third-party financial institution, keeping fees within the family.

The family had a great deal of implicit trust in this individual. We all viewed him as our advocate, our fiduciary, which extends beyond a typical service provider relationship. A fiduciary role entails that the professional must make decisions and take actions that are unconditionally in the best interest of the client. In contrast, other professionals such as broker-dealer financial advisors are not held to this standard.

The family office manager proposed a new SFO that would be a single investing entity for liquid and illiquid investments, with sleeves for various asset classes. (A sleeve is a group of investments, a subset of a portfolio, such as for different strategies or risk profiles.) In theory, this allows family capital to be pooled. This can be beneficial in terms of being able to access certain private investment funds that may have minimum requirements or economies of scale. Instead of three sets of financing documents to review and process and manage, there is one. It also allows the family principals to lend and borrow to and from other family members instead of from an outside bank. Practically speaking, we were signing up for at least a decade of having capital tied together—an important factor to consider when entering into such arrangements.

The family members would seek different asset allocations and different specific managers. We might gain access to managers or make deals with larger investment minimums than any sole investor could access. The administrative costs might be lower than what we'd been paying with the MFO, the trade-off being that it would be difficult to exit our liquid sleeves and near impossible to exit our illiquid sleeves.

The executive function of our family office would be outsourced to our manager. The family principals didn't have the time to lead the FO ourselves at the time. This outsourced leadership allowed for expertise beyond what the family had and is frequently seen in other offices.

We would insource our investing professionals, which is most effective when you have a large body of investing activity that needs internal management. The level of control and service are theoretically superior in this situation, but it pits family members against the established investing entities such as venture capital and private equity shops that can generally hire the best talent and are accustomed to paying top dollar.

> You should only bring something in-house if you have the capacity to do it well.

Finally, we'd set up that family bank of sorts. This would allow intrafamily loans to lessen the need for outside loans. It would minimize interest payments to nonfamily, yet again it would be difficult when one or more family members desired to exit the structure.

Whether you choose to insource these functions into your family office or contract out for them depends heavily on your needs and your purpose, and the services will be highly customized either way. Generally, you should only bring something in-house if you have the capacity to do it well. Be thoughtful about your needs far into the future, not just now, and think about whether it will be better implemented by in- or outsourcing that function.

Table 4.2. Our Specific SFO Feature Set

FEATURE	RATIONALE	ADVANTAGES	DISADVANTAGES
Unified overarching investing entity for liquid and illiquid investments, with sleeves for various asset classes	Under assumption that all family members would keep capital intact for at least a ten-year period, this model allows for different members to pursue different asset allocations	May gain access to managers or deals with larger investment minimums than any sole investor could access; lower administrative costs (theoretically)	Difficult to exit liquid sleeves; near impossible to exit illiquid sleeves; bookkeeping is complex
In-house investing professionals	Have a large body of investing activity that needs day-to-day management	Control and service levels are theoretically superior	Pits family against established entities that generally can hire the best
Outsourced specialists	Want best in class but don't have enough work for full-time	Professionals who work on many different FOs, bring broad industry knowledge	More costly on a per-hour basis than insourcing; marginal diminished service levels
Family bank	Allow intrafamily loans to provide easy liquidity	Minimize interest payments to nonfamily entities	Difficult when one or more family members need to exit structure

The Failed Pivot

Around this time, my brother began discussing whether to sell the family business. This would mean a large influx of cash, and the family office would be managing that capital. To my father's credit, he liked to play devil's advocate and would sometimes ask tough questions about the family's wealth. Around this time, during our Sunday afternoon check-in calls, he'd say something like, "The family office is soon going to be managing a lot of liquid capital. How might that change things?"

It was a fair question, and indeed, we believed we had the right structure. What I witnessed in our family and what I have heard about in other families is a natural occurrence when the older generation is transitioning the decision-making to the next generation: periodic hesitation on the part of the older generation. I didn't take it personally, but I wanted to instill confidence in my father so that he could let go, little by little, and trust us.

"Dad, we got this," I said. "You can hand us the reins."

The older generation has a natural tendency to hold on to the reins too long. This is a mostly universal theme, to the detriment of the younger generation, who is learning and taking responsibility. At the same time, this was a wise question posed by my father. I don't know if the younger generation—my siblings and I—had adequately thought through every scenario, which is often the case.

Also at this time, I developed a strong interest in sustainable investing through my day job at ONE WORLD. At times, I'd play with the idea of breaking off from the family office, moving my liquid investments out of the joint structure, and having more latitude to invest sustainably. And this is what I eventually ended up doing, yet mentioning it to my father never went over well.

"If it ain't broke," he'd say, "don't fix it." At the same time, his health was starting to deteriorate, and I could tell he was less focused on business and financial issues and more on his health, naturally. There was also a good deal of inertia with the current structure and players. Any change would be time consuming and would require a lot of work.

We put in place the series LLC model to enable different family lines to have different ownership interests in various asset classes and sustainable investing sleeves as well. In concept this was a good idea, if you assume it will be in place for a long period of time; in our case, as we chose to unwind it only a few years later, it was complex and costly to do so. For the moment, we, as a family, continued along with the same structure.

When examining a new or revised structure, it is important to realize the explicit and implicit assumptions that are made. For example, it was assumed that both my siblings would want to be part of the model for a decade or longer and that they wanted to be locked up in long-term investments. These assumptions proved to be incorrect. It was also assumed that our nonfamily manager was going to be in the family's picture for many years. As I understood it, there was no succession plan for the manager and no backup plan should he fall ill or decide it was time to move on or if some or all of the family decided they didn't want to work with him or the structure that he had created for the family.

When your family needs to evaluate its path forward, I recommend giving sufficient thought to the first key decision: building a separate SFO versus utilizing an MFO or virtual family office model. In our case, we assumed the SFO was better.

The family might have conducted more benchmarking with other family offices. While I recall a couple of conversations with one or two others, ideally, we'd have reviewed at least five and seen a variety of options. Family office networks (several are mentioned in the appendix D), especially those that are designed for the principals, are especially valuable tools here.

Families also need to give thought to how the family needs will evolve—skate-to-where-the-puck-will-be kind of thinking. What would happen if your family business were sold? What will happen as G3 comes of age? How will unfortunate situations—death, divorce, and so on—be handled?

Trusts

Another important structural tool is the trust. Trust funds are important financial planning vehicles that may contain liquid capital, stocks, bonds, a business, property, or other assets for an individual, group, or organization. They are established by a grantor on behalf of the beneficiary and are managed by trustees, which can be individual banks but are always neutral third parties.

Establishing a trust fund provides advantages for both the grantor and the recipient, including protection of assets, support for beneficiaries, avoidance of the probate process, and certain tax benefits, to name a few. Trusts will become particularly important as the older generations transfer mass amounts of wealth—$84 trillion through 2045 by one estimate—to the next generation in what is known as the Great Wealth Transfer. Around $72.6 trillion will be passed directly to heirs, and ultra-high-net-worth families, those in the top 1.5 percent, will be responsible for 42 percent of this transition.[1]

I spoke with Tavan Pechet, the CEO of Pechet Advisors, about trusts. To oversimplify, as he put it, instead of parents giving assets to a child to spend, the parents (or other grantors) give the assets to someone they trust (the trustee) to hold and manage on behalf of the child (or other beneficiary). There can be any number of grantors, trustees, and beneficiaries. The trustee holds and distributes these assets according to the terms of a document prepared by the grantor, so the parent gets to decide things like how much money the beneficiary gets, for what, and when—or they can empower the trustee to make these decisions.

There are many different types of trust funds, each with their own purpose and features. These include asset protection, blind, generation skipping, land, Medicaid, special needs, testamentary, and more. All trusts, however, can be categorized into one of two groups: revocable and irrevocable. A revocable trust, or living trust, is more flexible, which allows the grantor to alter or even revoke it before their passing. With this type of trust, the grantor can be the trustee themselves. Irrevocable trust funds, on the other hand, are difficult to change or make void, an arrangement that is inflexible but can also lead to significant tax benefits. A grantor is typically not a trustee in this case.

In an effort to fully understand how trusts interact with other legal entities that your family office may have, and ultimately tie back to individuals, I might suggest creating an entity map, as I have, to help visualize and understand the relationships.

Figure 4.1. Family Entity Map

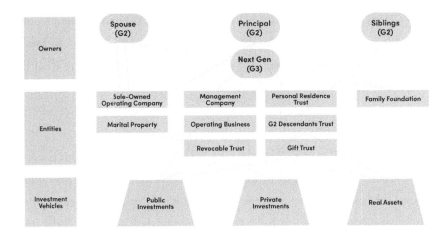

Refining the SFO

Because the single family office structure eventually no longer met our needs and because the manager transitioned out about two weeks after my father passed, G2 began moving to a hybrid situation: each sibling and their children would set up unique structures to manage certain functions and would also continue to manage some of the family-wide entities to administer other types of assets. We recognized that we all had different needs and goals for our respective family office services going forward and decided to consciously uncouple from each other. We each chose our own team of providers, although a few of them would overlap, and we started the migration of capital into our respective accounts.

My sister chose to work with a great new RIA who could provide back-end support of her affairs, and she chose to forgo setting up a family office structure. A dedicated family office doesn't need to be set up in each and all scenarios, and not having the structure, complexity, and additional costs made more sense for her.

My brother and I believed it made sense to have formal family office structures. We were familiar with setting up and managing companies; we both planned to actively manage a material amount of our capital directly, and we both had operating companies to complement the investing entities. We each created a somewhat hybrid approach—hiring some folks internally and working with our own set of advisors in complementary fashion.

Embracing my entrepreneurial inclinations, as I started to design my family office from scratch, I knew I'd be challenging these core assumptions and going in a different direction. As I saw it, having a de facto family office purpose, which is focused on growing capital, as most do, is too narrow and both leaves opportunity on the table and leads to a less sustainable family office. In my situation, I was embarking on setting up a new family office structure and felt lucky: not everyone gets a blank slate to set up their family office exactly as they like.

Setting up new businesses was something I was familiar with. Just a few years prior, I had set up my ONE WORLD business, the seventh start-up in which I have been part of the founding team. I had more than enough on my plate, and to be honest, I somewhat resented that I had to also figure out the family office part (high-class problems, to be sure). I was working a ton on my business and then trying to also fit in the family office at night and on weekends. You'll recall that I eventually aligned the family office with ONE WORLD, turning a problem into an opportunity.

With my purpose and vision set, it was time to engage the professionals to stand up the business entities required. Working with an attorney with significant expertise setting up family office structures at a national law firm, we came up with the following structure:

Figure 4.2. ONE WORLD Investments Organization Structure

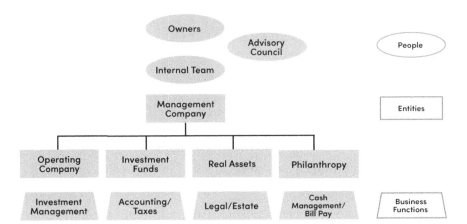

Owner

We decided that it was best for me to be the sole owner, at least for now. In the future, my spouse and our children could potentially become co-owners.

Management Company

We decided, with the guidance of outside family office attorneys, to have a management company contract for services as needed and serve as the core legal entity managing capital and also managing other ONE WORLD entities, including our training and consulting company.

Investment Vehicles

We created various LLCs to manage different classes of assets—public securities, private investments, alternatives, and so on. Each of these LLCs may own various proportions of different funds and assets. It is good practice to put any asset—from art to a fund—into an LLC to provide creditor protection, protection from changes like losing a partner or splitting from a comanager. In essence, each investor or trust would be able to have their own asset allocation, and if a specific investor wanted an asset class that they alone desired, that could be achieved as well. LLCs allow us the level of flexibility and customization we require.

Creating a one pager of this structure, and another with the specific trusts and LLC as well, has helped various family members internalize the structure and capital flows. Additionally, I have a much larger document I refer to as the "family office playbook" (see appendix A), with sections on open issues, the team, the calendar, asset distribution, a reporting template, an entity map, insurance, and so on.

I created the playbook for my own sanity but also as a contingency-planning safeguard, so that should my spouse or trustees have to take control of the family office in my unexpected unavailability, they could have all the key information in one place. Don't forget to update the playbook from time to time, and make sure the right people can access the document in case of an emergency.

This all comes back to that advice I keep repeating: manage the family office professionally, like any other business in terms of governance, goal setting, reporting, investing in the proper team, and collaborating with external professional service providers. Its structure flows from the needs of the customers—family—and the purpose it establishes. Careful thought and planning before creating any new LLC or investing the first dollar will help your family office sustain through many generations.

This Is Starting to Feel like a Job

In my conversations with several other family office principals, there is a theme that keeps emerging: having a family office is a job that requires more time and expertise than most believe it will, at least initially.

I have heard story after story of family office principals reflecting on how much time and effort the family office requires of them, and how they wish they were better prepared to manage the entity. In many cases, the division of labor among family members is not as clear as it could be, and in some cases, the workload is not equally split. This can cause family friction and resentment. The uneven split invites a moral hazard; family members sometimes think that other family members are watching the shop, so they can focus elsewhere, and they incorrectly believe that any risk is borne by all versus a single member. If everyone shares this mindset, it means that no one is watching the shop, properly managing things. It leads fairly quickly to problems—poor decisions on leadership, poor investment decisions by financial advisors, poor upkeep of the family assets such as shared vacation properties, underinsured assets such as shared family art collections, and any number of other issues. Complacency can be extremely destructive.

> Running a family office is a job that requires time and effort, and some key elements don't function well when they are outsourced to nonfamily members.

From my conversations with other family offices, the family principals' mindset is critical to get right from the start. The family has to be intimately involved in determining the structure and the players and in clarifying which family members are responsible for what elements. After all, a single family office is a business and of high importance—perhaps the most important—to the family. As all businesses need proper management and oversight, the family needs to internalize the fact that they are the ultimate managers of this business. It's a job that requires time and effort, and some key elements don't function well when they are outsourced to nonfamily members. If the family is not up to the task, then perhaps an MFO is a better choice, but that still requires having a hand on things.

A good deal of family office principals don't think the family office should have any external-facing mission, and few see it as requiring the same amount of effort as other businesses they may have managed. I believe this to be a problem that results in under-resourcing the family office. There are a few reasons for this. Burnout is especially common when the family office principal is currently running or recently ran a sizable operating company. They have run a business entity and want (likely need!) a break before jumping fully into the family office. Conversely, many family office principals have never worked in a business entity. Those that have may have worked in very different business types from what is required of a family office. They may also lack interest. Some principals are happy not having the responsibility and involvement, see their relationship as more at arm's length, and in some cases aren't explicitly or implicitly welcomed into the family office operations.

All of this leads to the family office struggling, which can be devastating to the principals who rely on it, not to mention future generations. This is why many family offices fail to last beyond a generation or two. To sustain your own family office, you will need to fully commit to running it professionally. Indeed, time, effort, and proper training to manage the managers are essential to provide for the principals.

In the end, the structure you choose for your family office is whatever works best for you. Whether that means a fairly simple model through a multifamily office or dedicating yourself full-time to managing a single family office, it must be designed to benefit your family principals. Each situation is unique, and so too should be the solution set of practices. Because the family's needs are dynamic, a periodic review and refresh of the current structure is necessary. The office is not a one-and-done project to set up and then just let it run on autopilot; it is a living organism you'll need to care for if you want it to thrive.

WHAT WORKS

- Gradual yet continual improvement of the family office structure—in our case, from an embedded office inside of the family business to an MFO and then to an SFO as the family needs evolve

WHAT DOESN'T

- Not having a succession plan in place for the family office CEO; this is a must-have

CHAPTER 5

Leadership

"Guys, what's the update with the family office?" asked my father one Sunday night when all the G2 siblings were at his house for pizzas and Grey Goose and tonics. It was a nice humid summer day at Dad's place in the suburbs. The baseball game was on as it often was in the background. We gathered for drinks and discussed at a high level what the update was. Our outside manager, who was starting to create our first single family office, had presented his plan and was in the process of executing it, building partnerships with asset managers and other service providers.

The manager proposed to be our quarterback. Like any good Midwestern family, we all loved football in our house, and sports metaphors ran rampant. He would oversee the creation of the new entities to run our office and bring in great outside financial managers to look after the capital.

Whereas most CEOs of a family business—whether G1 or subsequent—enjoy and seek the best fit for top leadership positions in a family business, with single family offices, this is not typically the case. What is quite common is to see family principals hire an outside person to run the family office for them. This is understandable but still requires the principals to oversee the office and its key providers.

Understandably, a family office principal, especially one who has just experienced a significant liquidity event, wants to hire someone else to create and run the new single family office. After all, the principal has worked hard—in some cases, for decades—not only building a business of scale but also selling it. Naturally, they seek some time off and the ability to enjoy their success and the wealth that it brings. They are excited in some cases to jump into charity work or to become an investor in the field in which they worked or a director on a board or to simply chill or travel. They know how to hire good people; they hired throughout their time in the family business. And they know how to manage them.

However, as revealed through my conversations with other family office principals, it is critical—especially in the early days of a new SFO structure—that each family principal remains very involved, if not as CEO themselves. While it may be tempting to ease into chairman of the board, which may be appropriate after things are up and running, they shouldn't fall into that role and mindset, at least not yet. Ideally, the principals will benefit from at least one annual cycle with a new or significantly altered structure under their belts before delegating significantly.

The type of professional who would be a good candidate to run the SFO depends on the scope of the SFO. If the SFO is principally focused on investing, then a financially savvy executive is ideal. Alternatively, if the SFO is broader in scope, as many are, then you'll need a leader who is good at multiple business functions.

It is important to call out that different family members will have different approaches to all things family office—in particular, who to hire and how long to keep them. With my father's health situation, he was spending less and less time on the family office, so it was becoming clear that we would soon need to designate new family leadership for it. We also needed to figure out how each of us would be involved going forward.

The Roles of the Family

A family office sounds straightforward until you stop to think about who is in the family, who is not, and among those who are in, whether they should be equally treated in terms of rights and access to assets. In my family, things started out pretty simple. As I mentioned earlier, my father (G1) decided to pass a portion of nonvoting family business shares equally to the G2 family members (that's me and my siblings). Voting shares were retained by G1 until he became removed from operating decisions, and then those were passed to the G2 sibling who was in the business (my brother). Other family assets that G1 created and managed—a vacation property and other nonfinancial assets—were similarly passed to G2 equally.

And so it was for a number of years, without issue. Looking back, and with the benefit of hearing how other families manage such issues, I realize that my father was making all such decisions himself; he hadn't explained to his children the logic and rationale of such decisions. In the event of my father's unexpected death or disability, we would not have benefited from his perspective and, perhaps, would not have been able to carry out his wishes with respect to how certain assets were managed into the future. We had a benevolent dictator who remained healthy for a long time; it doesn't always happen this way.

Our role in the family business also varied among G2. One of my siblings was running it; neither I nor the third sibling were in the business at all. I understood I was a beneficiary by virtue of the nonvoting shares I owned, but it was also clear that I had no input on any governance or management issues at the operating company at all. I didn't have any problem with this and didn't feel it was unfair in any way—until I started to think about how things might work once my father completely relinquished his role in the business.

At some of the family business conferences we attended, we would hear about situations where family members came and went in the family business and how this works and doesn't work as the generations unfold. For example, while I had decided against entering the family business, what about my children (G3)? Would they have the same opportunity as the children of my sibling who was running the business? What would happen if my sibling who was in the business decided to do something else? Would he retain all the voting shares and decisions, or would those revert to all G2 family members pro rata? Fortunately for us, the family avoided challenging situations that could have caused a lot of interfamily strife, but in hindsight, better clarification of which family members were making what decisions on family assets could have avoided all that worry.

That clarity is crucial, no matter what role each family member ends up playing in the family office. As I've said before, I recommend that every family member serve some role in the office. That role may vary from outright leadership to a minor operational role, but the more involved the better. I don't recommend the silent beneficiary end of the spectrum of involvement, but it is pretty common in practice. With privilege comes responsibility. There are low-impact ways to be an aware and engaged principal, to allow time to pursue your primary role in life if not in the family office. But the more involved you are, the better you can help guide the family office to best serve the broader family as well as your own family line.

Starting with the highest level of commitment, every family office needs a CEO. This person is in charge of high-level strategy, and they are the central connection for the people and partners of the family office. They oversee key functions, such as investing, taxes, and legal concerns. They hire and manage the rest of the family office team. This person must be able to manage multiple work streams and should have excellent skills in investing, reporting, and managing specialists. The CEO must also commit fully to the family office; this is a full-time position, not a nights and weekends job.

Next on the ladder is the director or manager level. These people lead specific divisions or functions; they might be the head of the family foundation or the manager of the family's venture capital fund. They should be knowledgeable in their specific area or function; they must be able to effectively lead teams and work together with other divisions, and they should have a strong desire to become the best in their class. This position also requires a hefty commitment of anywhere from ten to forty hours per week.

The chairperson manages the board or advisory council. They also hire, manage, and fire the CEO, so they should fully understand the purpose, vision, and values of the office and should be prepared to enforce them. They act as an executive liaison with key providers and partners, and they should be able to connect and integrate various family members' interests, as well as to recruit top talent. Although this is a crucial position, it may only require a commitment of around five hours per week.

Board members participate in operating reviews, provide a voice where appropriate, and must stay informed. They should have moderate expertise in understanding financial statements, and they should stay informed on key milestones and performance indicators for the family office. They will also participate in selecting nonfamily executives and managers. Being on the board requires only around one or two hours per week.

Finally, a family member may simply be a member. Even then, they'll need to stay informed; they should read their reports and attend all meetings, and they should always vote. They may be asked to professionally represent the office, and they should seek ways to strengthen it. In order to be a good member of the family office, they'll need a basic understanding of hiring and managing service providers, networking, and benchmarking with other family offices.

Table 5.1. Typical Roles for Family Office Principals

	CHAIR-PERSON	BOARD MEMBER	CEO	DIRECTOR / MANAGER	MEMBER
Responsibilities	Manages the board; hires, manages, and fires the CEO; executive liaison	Operating reviews; a voice where appropriate; stays informed	Strategy; people; partners; key functions	Leads specific division or function	Stays informed: reads reports, attends meetings, always votes; represents the office; seeks ways to strengthen the office
Essential skills	Ability to integrate various interests, recruit top talent	Expertise in financial statements, staying informed; nonfamily executive selection and management	Hiring and managing team; managing multiple work streams; investing, reporting, management of nonfamily specialists	Expertise in specific area or function; ability to function in team environment; ambition	Understanding how to hire and manage service providers; networking and benchmarking with other family offices
Hours per week	5+	1-2	40+	10-40+	2-3

The Right Stuff

The chairman position is typically most effective with a family principal in this role, especially if the CEO is a nonfamily professional. I also believe strongly that every family member should be somewhere on this table. At times, I will see situations where the principals are not even engaged as an observer; they are truly in the dark and unable to be effective when situations may evolve that require their involvement.

Any principal needs certain skills and knowledge to contribute to the future sustainability of their family office, and those requisites are more crucial the further up the leadership ladder you go. You must either have these skills yourself or hire people who do.

All family office principals need a basic understanding of finance and investing. They should understand asset classes, allocation, and risk. They should also understand what the leadership of their family office is doing, how much they are charging, and how well they perform. They should understand estate planning and should know how it affects the family business, the family office, and their own individual estate. Finally, they should understand the family's philanthropic efforts. They need to know why the family commits to certain causes, as well as how and how much.

Table 5.2. Family Office Principal Baseline Expertise: Questions Every Family Office Principal Should Know

CATEGORY	QUESTIONS EVERY FAMILY OFFICE PRINCIPAL SHOULD KNOW
Management and team	• How is the management performing in their role? What does their talent development plan look like, and who holds them accountable for building skills? • Are there any current or expected open roles? Who is responsible for recruiting them? • How is each key service provider doing? Any material changes at their firms that need to be discussed?
Finance and investing	• In general, what are the main asset classes, and what does each one provide to the overall portfolio in terms of risk and return? • Given risk tolerance and cash flow needs, what is the appropriate asset allocation? • Specific to one's net worth, what do the high-level income statement, balance sheet, and cash flows look like? • What benchmarks—both asset allocation, and manager fund specific—are used and why? • For each of the recent historical periods (annually or quarterly), what is the attribution analysis of over or under performance? Why did the portfolio behave a specific way, and are any changes being made as a result of this insight? • How much am I paying others to manage my investments? Which managers are earning what bps? Is that in line with the market? Are there other fees I pay that I should know about? Are any of my investment fees deductible? • How do my financial goals play into my broader goals for my capital? What are those broader goals? Are there additional ways I could be leveraging my capital to achieve my nonfinancial goals?

continued

Tax/accounting/ legal	· How much capital is in my estate currently? How much has been passed along to the next gen? · How much capital gains/ordinary income do I pay in a typical year? · Are we using a general ledger to manage all the flows of capital? · What are our largest sources of legal exposure and how are we managing them?
Estate planning	· What does the estate plan call for? Has it been revisited in the last five or so years by both the family principal and estate attorney to ensure it is still current? · Who are the trustees I have chosen for each trust? Are they aware of their role and my expectations in that role? Do we have periodic check-ins to discuss the trusts, their financial performance to the extent they hold financial assets, and the evolution of the beneficiaries of the trust?
Philanthropy	· What do I give in a typical year? Is this the proper amount, given my net worth and my desires? · What vehicles does the family utilize for philanthropic giving—a family foundation and/or donor-advised fund (DAF)? Does it make sense to explore alternative vehicles given our goals, such as a 501(c)4, or a special purpose trust (SPT)? What are the pros/cons of these options? · How is the endowment of the family foundation or the assets at a DAF being invested? Is it being invested in alignment with our philanthropic goals? Are we utilizing mission-related investing (MRI) or program-related investing (PRI)? Why or why not?

When I created my own SFO, I knew I would be its CEO. And while I had been CEO of several operating companies, it was the first time I was CEO of a family office, and I needed to evaluate my own skill set and possibly complement my skills with those of other people. Beyond the obvious pockets of expertise (investing, accounting, bill pay), what capabilities did I need to have to power this office? And given my decision to merge the family office with the operating companies, how did that affect our needs?

I leaned on what has always been successful for me with my other start-ups, and that was the formation of an advisory council for the family office. I outlined the capabilities I needed to achieve the vision into a few key categories: investing, legal, general knowledge about the family office, entrepreneurship, and social impact. Then I started to think about which individuals I knew directly, knew of, or felt I could enlist on this journey. I put together a wish list that would ultimately become my advisory council. Next, I created an overview of what I wanted this council to do and how often it would connect (see appendix B).

The council is composed of five individuals. Most crucial, they have the knowledge I need to build and manage what I envision for the long-term family office, but they also have zero conflicts of interest. Tempting as it may be to include, for example, a financial manager who may provide services to your family office, resist or at least make it clear that, as part of the advisory council, there will not be the potential to engage in paid work beyond the council. That said, I do strongly believe in compensating my council with an annual fee in order to get the best talent and, of course, paying all out-of-pocket fees (e.g., travel to meetings). We meet quarterly, and since most members are outside of my state, three of the four meetings are virtual and one is an in-person two-day meeting each year.

We are three years in, and the value of the advisory council has been remarkable. They help me set the right priorities, think through strategy, and push back when I am off course. They help challenge my key assumptions and help me manage the managers by pointing out what is industry standard and, in many cases, by making introductions to expertise I wouldn't have found otherwise. And they motivate me and help to keep me accountable for staying focused on executing the goals of the organization.

So I knew my role, and I knew I'd stand up an advisory council, but what about all the other roles? While it was a bit challenging to think this step through in the absence of the providers I was already working with, it was worthwhile. I didn't want momentum to simply carry me forward with legacy service providers that weren't a fit.

Figure 5.1. ONE WORLD Ecosystem

I had to decide whether I would hire these providers directly or whether I would outsource them. If I created an insourced team, these individuals would be dedicated employees of my family office, with a singular focus on its needs. I'd have control over our priorities and focus, and we could build trust, institutional knowledge, and camaraderie together. However, I'd have to make sure I had enough work to keep a team occupied, and I'd have to manage them. They wouldn't necessarily have the ability to see across multiple client situations as an outsourced professional would. If I hired outside professionals or firms, they would be working for multiple clients, including me. That would mean less attention probably, but it would also mean that they'd draw experience from multiple situations, and my office could benefit from that knowledge. Outsourcing entails more flexibility, and I wouldn't have to manage anyone. The costs could either be lower, if I didn't need full-time employees, or more expensive if their services piled up. Outsourcing would typically be better if I decided to keep the office small and nimble; insourcing would support growth.

I created this table to help me think through where I wanted to insource talent into the family office structure and where I wanted to outsource it. These are not permanent decisions, but insourced talent can't be immediately terminated and also takes a while to secure, whereas outsourced providers are generally plentiful and more agile to hire and discontinue.

Table 5.3. Insource vs. Outsource for Core Family Office Roles*

*Core roles typically include investment management, accounting, tax advising, while other types of roles such as cooks, pilots, dog walkers, personal security have different considerations.

	INSOURCED	OUTSOURCED
Definition	Dedicated to your SFO (may be full-time or part-time)	Work for multiple clients, in addition to you
Pros	Control; Trust; Institutional knowledge	"Try before buy"; Flexibility to expand/contract easily; Cost (for part-time); Expertise
Cons	Management with a single view of family offices	More costly (for full-time)
Typically good if...	You have enough work; You value the camaraderie	You are smaller; You don't want to manage people; You like the flexibility

Female Family Principals

More than ever, women are taking on greater responsibilities and leadership roles in family offices. According to Morgan Stanley, almost one-third of family office executives are women, a rate that surpasses female leadership roles in the corporate sphere.[1] These trends reflect the overall pattern of women gaining increasing financial literacy and responsibility; nationally, women control a whopping $10.9 trillion, and that amount will only continue to increase as baby boomers pass on their assets to the next generation in the Great Wealth Transfer.[2] Several factors will contribute to women's growing share of financial control, including their longer life expectancy and the improved financial knowledge of the younger female generation.

Despite women's increasing financial power and influence, they still face obstacles and biases in the industry. Kristin Hull, CEO of Nia Impact Capital and executive of the Nia Family Office, says, "Women are often tasked with taking care of more mundane activities, such as planning offsite and other social activities, family meals, and other administrative tasks." They are less involved with family offices and more likely involved with a grants committee or impact investing than their male counterparts. "Historically, family wealth has often been generated by men in many families. The patriarchy in society can also play out at the family office level. Women tend to be called on less often in meetings and may also speak less than the men. The men do much of the speaking and tend to be placed in decision-making roles on invest committees working on asset allocation, etc."

One of the primary concerns is flagging self-confidence. According to a 2023 UBS survey, only 53 percent of women primary earners consider themselves "highly knowledgeable about investing," compared with 75 percent of their male counterparts.[3] Furthermore, a 2021 study published in the *Journal of Economic Behavior* showed that the misconception of women being "bad with money" contributes to this discrepancy in confidence.[4] Advisor relationships can also be fraught for women, with 64 percent of female primary earners surveyed in the UBS study saying that the financial industry has been patronizing to women, with those same-sex couples feeling even less supported.[5]

However, there is plenty of evidence supporting women's ability to excel in leadership. Hull says, "We know from the research that diverse teams make better-quality decisions, often resulting in a higher ROI. The research tells us that women make good investors. Also, commonly, family offices struggle to engage all family members, which can result in tricky and difficult family dynamics. When half of all members are not given equal representation, that can certainly tear at the seams of the office . . . Leaving out female principals in family offices may mean leaving untapped talent at the door, can lead to interfamily strife, and may also be leaving money on the table."

Clearly, there is still work to be done to ensure that women feel more self-assured and accepted as they gain a greater share of financial responsibility in family offices and beyond. There are several important ways to help them feel empowered and supported: First, it is crucial to promote gender diversity in hiring practices. It is particularly important for young women professionals to see female representation among the principals and to have the opportunity to work with female leaders. Second, families of multigenerational wealth should focus on equal inclusion and education among their sons and daughters; this engagement early on can encourage both genders of the next generation to become involved in the long term. Next, quality governance structures give female family members the opportunity to have their voices heard so decision-making can incorporate their concerns and opinions. Finally, men need to become allies in this journey by supporting their female coworkers and family members, actively inviting their input, serving as mentors, and genuinely listening to and respecting their desires and goals.

These measures can help foment change not only within family offices but in the world at large, as many women have a desire to use their financial resources with purpose to achieve positive impacts in their sectors of interest. Another UBS survey from 2020 showed that for 72 percent of women in the study, the events of the last several years have sparked a desire to "make more of a difference in the world," with millennials demonstrating the highest level of aspiration. Additionally, 92 percent believe that "being involved in long-term financial planning can enable me to make more of an impact."[6] Their areas of interest include education, environment, poverty, social justice, and more.

Empowering women in family offices and in the investments your family office chooses to make not only benefits the family itself and their future generations by incorporating women's contributions and ideas but also the world at large through their dedication to making a difference.

"Women are more likely to want to bring a conscious lens to investing," says Kristin Hull. "They often seek to understand where their money sleeps at night and what types of impacts their dollars are having on both the environment and their communities." Clarifying where your money sleeps at night—how your funds are being invested, what industries and companies benefit from your capital—and how that aligns

> Clarifying where your money sleeps at night—how your funds are being invested, what industries and companies benefit from your capital—and how that aligns with your values is an important step toward taking full control of your capital.

with your values is an important step toward taking full control of your capital. When an investment opportunity fails to align with the family office purpose, "female family office principals will likely raise their voice more than their male counterparts. Women are more likely to go deep in terms of assessing teams or company collaborations for due diligence, which only helps returns as well as value alignment."

The first step to increasing inclusion for women in family offices, according to Hull, is to approach the situation as you would any inclusion issue: "Have an honest conversation." You can also hire a change-management professional to help shift the office's representation. "Ideally, all members have input into the plan, and all members have a role moving forward . . . Education on investing and family office management is always helpful—not just for females, of course. In some family offices, I have seen formal mentor relationships (between say an aunt and a niece) that are facilitated to help educate the younger generation, and this can be done in a way that empowers younger women to learn from older women." Including more women in family office leadership means more cohesion among the principals, but it also means more ideas from a wider group of stakeholders, which usually means better outcomes for everyone.

WHAT WORKS

- The principals should be as involved as possible in running the family office, especially in the early days

- Principals should be aware, curious, and attentive about how the office is doing and should participate in all meetings and votes

- An advisory council or board, with at least some nonfamily members, free of any conflicts of interest, that provides accountability, advice, and support

WHAT DOESN'T

- G1 holding on to all governance for too long can mean passing over the opportunity to engage and share wisdom with G2

- Cultures and practices that fail to fully engage women principals for their intelligence and ability to participate in family office leadership

PART 2

BUILDING THE FAMILY OFFICE

To be effective, family office principals have to become experts at sorting through huge amounts of information and knowing what's important and what's not. To run the office, you need to understand that you can only succeed by clearly communicating with your service providers or managers. An understanding of financial reporting is important—what has happened historically with the capital in the family office, and what actions going forward are recommended, if any. You'll see more paperwork and reports than you can count, and you'll want to check in with your expert managers, whether they are in-house or engaged from outside the family office.

Understanding the basic operations of the family office such as accounting and taxes is vital, as is having a working knowledge of technology that might help streamline the family office or make your work easier. You'll also want to be familiar with the risks involved in the family office and the costs it is likely to incur.

A huge part of a sustainable family office is its function of maintaining and even growing the family capital. That requires investment, which means you'll need to understand the basics of risk and reward, as well as the various asset classes common to investing at this scale.

Beyond how and how much to invest, many modern investors are also considering the impact that their investing has both now and potentially in the future. They want to make a positive change in the world, either through supporting businesses and investments that either do no harm or that directly benefit the world in some way; this is sustainable and impact investing.

You don't have to be an expert in each of these fields, but knowing enough to understand the issues facing the office and to make informed decisions is crucial.

CHAPTER 6

Performance Management

The amount of information a family office principal receives is staggering. You'll receive annual, quarterly, and monthly reports; one-time updates; and transactions from a wide variety of sources, including registered investment advisors (RIAs), custodians, attorneys, federal and state entities, fund managers, and other specialists. That is still probably only a fraction of what is available to see. I work with an open inbox policy. I ask that everyone copy me on any and all reports but also flag those that require action (a signature, approval, etc.). On a tactical level, I have created a dedicated email address for all notices and reports. It is cloud based and secure so I have a backup. This is the bottom-up way I process information.

If the sole concern of family members is that the family office make money, then perhaps the out-of-the-box reporting that you receive from your financial team can suffice. However, of all the family office members I have met, this is true in only a few cases. This is where a customized, top-down report becomes important. In my case, I created this summary report with my advisory council, who is familiar with not only the financial goals of my family office but also the broader set of goals we have established. The idea behind it was to think, "If I could only get one brief report each quarter, what would it report on?" Whittling down all the information into a meaningful one- or two-page report took a bit of effort, but it was an important forcing function to prioritize and determine what matters most.

Table 6.1. Capital Impact Report

CAPITAL			IMPACT					
Asset class	$	% Total	Financial			Impact		
			ITD	BM	+/-	% Trad.	% Sust.	% Impt.
Cash	$5	5%	0.8	0.8	n/a		100	
Fixed income	$25	25%	1.8%	2.0	-0.2%	50	50	
Public equity	$42	42%	11%	10%	1%		100	
Private equity	$18	18%	15%	17%	-2%	30		70
Real assets	$10	10%	8%	7%	1%	25	25	50
Total	$100	100%						

ITD - Inception to Date (becomes valuable after at least 2 years of data)
BM - Benchmark
% Traditional - % of asset class traditionally invested—no sustainable posture
% Sustainable - % of asset class sustainably invested—aligned with ESG goals
% Impact - % of asset class impact invested—invested in impact solution companies/funds

From this one page, I can understand the main asset allocation, how each class has performed since inception against the benchmark, and how each of those classes is invested on a scale of sustainability (from traditional to impact).

Determining your custom reporting is tightly linked to the purpose and vision activities. It is what will tell you how well you are achieving the purpose of your family office. If, like most, you have broader goals for your family office—to generate capital for philanthropic purposes or real estate or a sports team or an alpaca farm—the appropriate reporting can help.

Working with a variety of financial professionals from a range of firms over the years, one thing seems to always be true: there is way too much information in reports and way too few actionable recommendations. The reporting tends to be mostly if not exclusively looking in the rearview mirror rather than toward the future. Reports rarely offer unique information (thus the need for custom reporting), and they rarely include forward-looking projections and recommendations.

This is one place where the contrast between a family business and a family office is distinct. An operating business typically has robust business planning meetings and reporting requirements. They may be quarterly, and they focus on the mission of the organization, its key strategies and metrics to determine how well those are working. There are always plans for how to get from point A to point B, and for the investments and talent that are required to do so.

In the family office, planning meetings are much less common. The reports tend to be financial and historic in nature. This can limit our actionable insights. A helpful reporting process and the reports themselves should be easy to digest. It's great to have all the detail in the appendix, but the first pages, the ones that typically get the bulk of the readers' attention, should be simple and clear. All family office principals will profit from knowing both qualitatively and quantitatively how their investment team is doing and why.

Reporting involves periodic check-ins to ensure you're moving in the right direction and forecasting to see where you might be headed. Reports need to be connected to specific goals that the principals have; for example, if the family wants a certain amount in cash flow by a specific date to enable the family to purchase a vacation property, the reports should reflect progress toward that goal.

Out-of-the-box reports from financial professionals are often organized in ways that may make sense to your providers and professionals but not to you. Here is a simple example: if you consider your capital and that of your children to be separate—with separate goals, risk tolerances, cash needs, and thus investing strategies—then these should not be reported in the aggregate.

The whole point of reporting is to convey actionable information; if you don't understand something, don't stop asking questions until you do. Depending on the financial manager, their reports may be based on a template that is hard for the providers to change; I often hear the excuse that the external providers can't make changes due to limits from their compliance department. If this is the case with yours—if your reports lack some information that you feel you need—again, ask questions. Reporting is intended to adequately inform you to make decisions in the best interest of your family office, so make sure you understand it.

Every single family office principal should have an executive summary, in addition to reports that provide detail as required. This summary should be explicit enough to let you easily answer the following basic questions:

- How much capital do I own?
- What is the breakdown by major category (e.g., cash, fixed income, equity, private—liquid and nonliquid)?
- Where and how is the capital invested (i.e., which funds, which managers, ESG or sustainable)?
- How is the financial performance of the capital compared with benchmarks?

- What level of risk am I taking on in each asset class, and is this appropriate for my goals?
- How does the change in capital affect our overall goals for the year?

If you can answer these questions—even at a high level—you are well ahead of most other family office principals. Let's take a deeper look into each one.

Most family office principals have a ballpark sense of their "number"—an all-in figure of their total net worth. Obviously, with principals that have material shares of a privately held company or other private equity funds, it's a bit trickier to value. Your annual report should give you a much better idea of where each piece of the puzzle fits, even if it's just a snapshot.

You can break down the total in the same way a balance sheet does—by type of asset class. It is important to have a sense of which asset classes are liquid or could be liquid, if needed. A great many individuals are wealthy on paper but cash poor, and they have to sell assets in an untimely and expensive manner to fund their expenses. Being informed ahead of time will help you avoid that large haircut.

We must then look at which specific managers and funds make up the investment in a specific asset class. For example, for a family that has a large private equity portfolio, what are the specific positions? Which are funds and which are direct investments? How much is held in each? What are the remaining capital calls?

Many families also care deeply about the quality of the investments; you might ask, "What do those managers or companies I have put my capital into actually do?" "Am I investing in private prisons, tobacco companies, or weapons manufacturers, and if so, how do I feel about that?" This is where environmental, social, and corporate governance (ESG) analysis comes in, which oddly seems to have become a politically charged issue. Let me address this in as neutral a fashion as I can. If all you do is use ESG as a process to collect more information on a company or a fund, then that is value in and of itself. More data is always better data when it comes to evaluating an investment. Do the analysts think that a potential investment is risky from a climate perspective? If so, I'd think any investor would want to know.

Next, you'll need to work closely with your CIO to agree on which are the most relevant benchmarks. For asset classes such as cash, this is pretty easy. For other asset classes, such as public equity, this can become complex; there may be asset subclasses such as international growth equity that will roll up to a single benchmark for that class. While benchmarking each class is important, I am more concerned with the overall blended benchmark. Most financial professionals agree that asset allocation has an outsized impact on the long-term returns of a portfolio compared with the specific manager or asset selection.

How does the change in capital affect the annual goals of the family office? Well, to answer that, you first have to answer this question: Do you have overall goals for the family office? Some do; some don't. If you have identified that one of the main goals for your office is to provide free cash flow to channel into philanthropy or to build up a capital base for a specific future acquisition, how well has the past period fared with that goal in mind?

One of the main goals of my own family office is providing support for sustainable investing in all asset classes and doing so at market rate returns. Some of the capital is still invested in traditional funds and with managers that aren't deemed to be sustainable investments, so it's a work in progress. But the point is that, at each reporting period, I need to know how well we are doing against that goal. The only way to measure our progress is to see both the goal and where you are, so you can make the best decisions to move you forward.

I am a visual learner—it's how I best absorb, learn, and recall information. This is something that took me many years to realize, but once I did, I began trying to take information presented one dimensionally and transform it into something that would be more useful to me in decision-making.

Financial reporting is a great example. Typically, financial advisors will produce reports that are mostly black and while, with text, tables, figures, and percentages. Occasional pie charts show asset allocation, or bar charts show growth over time. And for many, this may be sufficient.

However, for those like me who benefit from a more visual representation, there are many options. Take for example the below asset map which I use in understanding different owners of capital. The map is a simple 2 × 2 representation of assets placed along two axes that define the nature of the asset and the type of management by the owner. The x-axis is the private and public dimension, and the y-axis is the active and passive dimension.

Figure 6.1. Asset Map

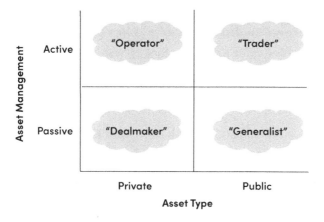

Among other things, I use this framework to think about how my family capital is allocated and how that compares with the time and attention that I give to each of the quadrants. For example, for a family principal who spends the bulk of her time and energy on evaluating and making direct investments (lower left) but has 90 percent of her wealth in public equities (lower right), she might pay more attention to the pubic equities to ensure the bulk of the capital is well managed. Often, there is a disconnect in where the assets lie and where the principal spends her time, or where the office has built out its expertise.

Remember, it all comes back to you, as the principal, needing to understand the family office's finances. If that means more details or different specifics in your forecasting, asking more questions of your managers, or having them present the report visually, make sure you receive the information in a manner that lets you make the best decisions for your family.

Forecasting and Modeling

You know the old disclaimer, "Past performance is not an indication of future performance"? I say, "Fine. Then, let's create our own forecasts." Of course you can't guarantee future performance, but the past can certainly inform your understanding of it. Once you have a few years under the belt, it becomes helpful to look at past years to then better forecast the future. You can do some basic financial modeling to help answer questions such as:

- What would happen if I doubled my philanthropic giving next year?

- How will it affect my financial position if I buy that piece of art or vacation property today? What about five years from today?

- I am thinking of selling a certain asset that has both financial and emotional value. What would it mean for my future assets, taxes, and so on if I sold it?

Forecasting is not only important from an accountability standpoint, but it also ties closely into your long-term goals and planning. It need not be complex to be useful. The following simple example of a system-level template includes all the basic pieces you can use to forecast.

Table 6.2. Forecasting Model for Investment Assets (Excludes Personal Assets Such as Houses, Artwork, Etc.)

YEAR	1	2	3	4	5
Starting capital	$100	$98	$100	$99	$97
Growth rate (appreciation plus interest plus dividends)	+7%	+7%	+7%	+7%	+7%
Material inflows and outflows: Year 2 - redemption of shares Year 4 - purchase vacation property		+$3		-$2	
Taxes	-2%	-2%	-2%	-2%	-2%
Fees	-1%	-1%	-1%	-1%	-1%
Expenses	-2%	-2%	-2%	-2%	-2%
Inflation	-4%	-3%	-3%	-2%	-2%
Ending capital	$98	$100	$99	$97	$97

The starting investment capital is a subset of your total net worth. For me, this includes only assets used as investments and not personal assets that I am unlikely to part with, such as my primary residence. The blended growth rate across all investment classes depends heavily on how aggressively those investment assets are positioned; 5 percent is likely a good starting point. The material inflows and outflows are what will materially change your picture. Of course, you can only forecast the elements you have visibility into, so clarity on those elements is important. Are you planning a major purchase in the coming years? Do you expect to sell off a nonliquid asset soon? Include those figures in your inflows. Taxes include both federal and state for a total. I look at this on a cash basis (what was actually paid) and not an accrual basis. Your fees are the total fees for your family for anything related to the family office. Do you know what you pay your various advisors and how that compares to benchmarks? You should know. Finally, I would also include your expenses: What are your family expenses, including philanthropy, household costs, domestic helpers, nannies, cooks, pilots, and so on? All of this information—some of which you can get from those annual and quarterly reports—is crucial for looking to the future. And if you have a financial professional reluctant to create a forecast, you need to convince them or find a new advisor.

The Quarterly Check-In

In many family offices, the quarterly review provides the main vehicle for the family and staff to connect and review performance and also provide status updates of other initiatives. In our family, simply scheduling the reviews was always a challenge, with everyone's busy schedules, extensive work, and personal travel. The meetings would typically start with some pleasantries as everyone would settle in. At times, small talk would extend for a good fifteen minutes, something that would not occur in a typical business meeting among outside professionals. The first agenda item would often be financial review, and the investment manager would often have dozens of pages of financial reports.

As we tried to walk through the pages, we'd inevitably get hung up on a smaller detail early in the report, missing the big picture or headlines of the review completely. Often the reporting templates would change from one period to the next, making historical comparisons challenging. This has been the case with each of the various investment managers I have worked with over the years, and it is apparently quite common.

We'd see large numbers in the total or net worth line items, generally feel warm and fuzzy about those figures, and—at least for myself—wouldn't ask too many questions for fear of looking uninformed in front of other family. But I had a good sense that they too understood only a small fraction of what was presented.

And then we'd move on to other issues—for example, where we were in the process of bringing on another provider, updates on family-owned personal assets, and so on. During the meeting, if any of the family members received a call, they'd pick up, and the rest of the participants would wait awkwardly until the seemingly trivial call ended. Inevitably, the meetings would go overtime; whether we scheduled them to be two hours or four hours, we'd run out of time.

In the spirit of learning, based on conversations with several other family principals, here is how these meetings could have gone: At least two weeks prior to the meeting, an agenda should have been set, with input from the family, and the proper amount of time should have been allocated to the meeting based on the time for each agenda item. Any materials to be reviewed at the meeting should have been sent out with the agenda, providing the attendees adequate time to review the documents. This communication packet should have included the minutes from the previous meeting, which would help the members recall open issues and key decisions to be made at the upcoming meeting.

On meeting day, a separate time should be allocated for the warm-up, to allow participants to socialize and catch up. For example, an informal lunch might be scheduled immediately before a one p.m. meeting start time. Norms should be established, if not also made explicit around how the meeting is conducted: Can one pick up a phone call? Can one leave early for a nonemergency? The manager has the responsibility to ensure that the meetings stay on track, start and end on time, and have an overall professional tone to them. Each family will determine what their specific norms and customs are. During the financial review, the family members should be helped to understand both benchmarking the asset allocation for investable assets, as well as benchmarking specific managers and funds or asset allocations. Time should be left in the meeting to provide a recap of the issues and decisions discussed and to be clear about the follow-up items, who is responsible for them, and what the next steps are. Time should be left in each meeting to discuss how the meetings are conducted: whether they are of the proper length, whether you should include other participants, and so on. And before breaking, the participants should agree to the dates and times of the next two or three meetings; some will find it helpful to schedule as far as one year out.

After the meeting, the manager should send a summary of the event to all participants the next day. It is also the manager's role to ensure that the meetings are something that the members look forward to, that they understand the importance of the meetings, and that they are fulfilling the needs of the various members.

Each family principal has the responsibility to obtain a baseline level of understanding about the concepts of finance, investing, accounting, and estate planning. This can be a multiyear journey, and no one can be expected to have this knowledge without proper training. Such a baseline will ensure they can participate in the meetings in a material way. It is part of the manager's job to ensure that each family member has access to resources to help provide this baseline level of education.

WHAT WORKS

- Having a one-page executive summary for financial performance, as well as other key metrics that should be tracked
based on the office's purpose

- Blending quantitative and qualitative reporting,
as appropriate

WHAT DOESN'T

- Principals allowing financial managers to provide moun-
tains of reports without actionable takeaways

- Family office meetings that lack proper planning and execution—no rereading materials, no norms around how the
meeting is conducted, etc.

CHAPTER 7

Operations

Distinct from the performance management functions of the family office, you'll also need to pay close attention to the financial operations, such as accounting and taxes. These are complicated topics that require some background education and trusted service providers. Technology can provide important tools for productivity and automation, but it can also leave you open to attack; you'll need to carefully plan ahead for any hacking event. Finally, this may seem simple, but many principals are not as aware as they need to be about the costs of running a family office. All of these crucial pieces will require your attention and a base level of knowledge.

Accounting

I have a confession to make: I find accounting a tad dry. When I learned the basics in college and then again in business school, it wasn't that I found any of the concepts too hard to grasp (perhaps with the exception of accounting for equity stock swaps), but the level of precision seemed way more daunting than the implication of the numbers. You too may find accounting less than thrilling. Tough cookies for us both! A fool and his money are soon parted, and a family office principal without a solid grasp of basic accounting will be proven a fool sooner or later.

As a single family office principal, you have to know how to read a balance sheet, income statement, and cash flow statement. You have to know what a receivable is, what negative retained earnings means, which expenses are deductible and which are not, and the difference between ordinary tax rates and capital gain rates. Obtaining this knowledge and staying on top of things is a cost of doing business as a single family office principal, and it will save you tons of money and time and angst.

Kelly Zurek, managing director of Andersen Private Accounting Solutions and former CFO for the Family Office Exchange (membership organization for family offices) and for a Chicago-based single family office, says, "It is critical that the family office principals match the right accounting and reporting talent to their needs. When a family office is starting out or represents only one generation of beneficiaries, its needs may be met by a more junior bookkeeper or accountant. As it grows—more complexity, more generations, etc.—then it requires more sophisticated accounting talent. Enterprise-type family offices, with diverse asset bases and many beneficiaries, require a CFO—way beyond the sole bookkeeper that a simple, early-stage family office can manage to get by with."

She continues, "Good planning requires understanding what talent is available to execute the plans. Sometimes this requires moving the accounting function out of a family business (where perhaps a corporate accountant could handle the work previously), to a dedicated structure with dedicated professionals who are hired for a specific purpose in the family office . . . You can't build a solid and successful family office on crumbling rock—you need a strong foundation, with the right people."

If you have never taken an accounting course or need to get a refresher on the basics, the tsunami of financial reports you will see might as well be written in a different language. You won't know what matters and what you can skim through. But there are tons of resources online, and you can have your financial manager sit and teach you the basics.

Taxes

Family offices spend a good amount of energy on tax planning, both for the short term and for the longer term. But please be sure that you don't let the tail wag the dog. My siblings and I, as co-owners of a family-held business, had the opportunity to pass ownership of some of the business shared from our estate down to our respective children. We proceeded under the thinking that passing highly appreciating assets was a smart estate planning move. Indeed it was—from just that one lens. However, the assets in question appreciated dramatically beyond our expectations, which resulted in a higher proportion of wealth at the younger generation than might be ideal as compared to the older generation. This imbalance has created some regret within the older generation ("giver's remorse," if you will). From a lesson's learned perspective, what I'd say to other family office principals is to give thought to the range of outcomes when passing assets to the next generation. How would you feel if the asset went to zero? If it appreciated twentyfold? While a potential gift or sale may be tax efficient, does it align with your goals and desires for you, your children, and the larger family office?

I am working on reframing how I think about paying taxes. In many investor circles—not just family offices—taxes are treated as sort of a necessary evil of doing business that needs to be shrunk as small as possible. For many, having to pay a million-dollar tax bill (or greater) can feel outlandish. And while, indeed, it may be a lot of money, I think it wise to put the figure into perspective. How fortunate are individuals who have made so much money that they get to write huge tax checks to the government? Talk about doing one's civic duty! The streets that we all use, the police we rely on, the public servants, space programs, public facilities—these happen only because such checks get written. And let's remember, when a million-dollar check is cut to pay taxes, a much larger amount stays with the principal whose investments generated that tax bill.

The tax advantages of a family office itself will depend on a number of factors. One is the ability to consolidate the management of the family's wealth, which can help reduce taxes, reduce administrative costs, and streamline tax reporting.

Paige Goepfert is a managing director of the Andersen Private Client Services team and works with ultra-high-net-worth families, family offices, business owners, and executives on tax planning and income tax compliance. Paige says that, "before considering the tax implications of a family office, family office principals are well served to think about the catalysts for and objectives of their family office. The structure, including how the management services are going to be provided and the type of entity formed for the management company, will determine the tax impact.

"A common mistake I see is when families initially contemplate forming a family office solely because of the tax benefits they hope to obtain. While there may be tax benefits from a family office structure, anticipated tax benefits should not be the catalyst for setting up a family office . . . We [also] sometimes see families stuck in a certain mindset even when their goals and tax laws are constantly changing. For example, an older family member may feel like they have already given too much to the next generation or their grandchildren and, on principle, will not consider what they are leaving on the table from a tax perspective . . . My role as an advisor [and this is why you should design your family office team well] is to help a client define their strategy and make sure the economic and tax implications are clearly understood before a final decision is made."

Firms like Paige's can help their clients streamline across traditionally separated business divisions. "For us, tax, accounting, and estate planning—these service offerings all work in unison toward broader goals. We try to help clients determine their strategy, their longer-term goals beyond simply making money, and then create the right operating system to help families achieve those goals."

Family Office Technology

Family office technology is in a state of both high growth and high demand. Providers are competing in a rush to innovate and capture their user bases; according to Simple's 2023 Family Office Software and Technology Review, such software firms have consistently indicated strong growth over the previous three years.[1] Meanwhile, 54 percent of the family offices surveyed answered that they do not currently use family office–specific software. From a cost standpoint, IT and tech account for about 5 percent of family office internal operations, and 49 percent of offices think their IT or tech spending costs will increase in the next three years.[2] Clearly, there is much room to grow, and firms are eagerly taking advantage of this opportunity.

Tech integration can greatly enhance family office efficiency. It falls into three major value chain segments: aggregation, management and analysis, and reporting.[3] Some US-based examples include Black Diamond Wealth Platform, Ledgex, Nines, and Canopy. Family offices, for their part, demonstrate a strong desire for tech adoption, with top demands from family offices including integration of features like onboarding, portfolio analysis, and reporting; platform customization and ease of use; data security and privacy (encryption, multifactor authentication, firewalls, etc.).

Figure 7.1. What Are the Top 5 Demands from Your Clients?

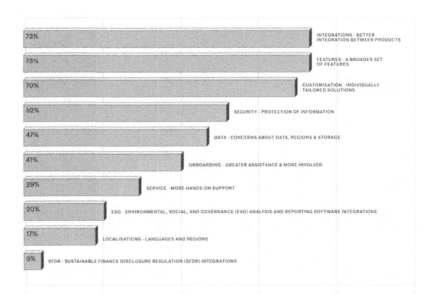

INTEGRATIONS - BETTER INTEGRATION BETWEEN PRODUCTS — 73%

FEATURES - A BROADER SET OF FEATURES — 73%

CUSTOMISATION - INDIVIDUALLY TAILORED SOLUTIONS — 70%

SECURITY - PROTECTION OF INFORMATION — 52%

DATA - CONCERNS ABOUT DATA, REGIONS & STORAGE — 47%

ONBOARDING - GREATER ASSISTANCE & MORE INVOLVED — 41%

SERVICE - MORE HANDS-ON SUPPORT — 29%

ESG - ENVIRONMENTAL, SOCIAL, AND GOVERNANCE (ESG) ANALYSIS AND REPORTING SOFTWARE INTEGRATIONS — 20%

LOCALISATIONS - LANGUAGES AND REGIONS — 17%

SFDR - SUSTAINABLE FINANCE DISCLOSURE REGULATION (SFDR) INTEGRATIONS — 5%

Source: Simple Research & Data - https://andsimple.co/.

Cybersecurity is at center stage, as 36 percent of global family offices surveyed in 2022 had experienced one or more cyberattacks over the previous twelve months.[4]

At the same time, family offices face significant barriers in expanding their tech integration. Resourcing can be particularly challenging; in the BlackRock 2022–2023 Global Family Office Report, 53 percent of family offices surveyed indicated that they recognize gaps in technology resourcing and expertise.[5] Tech lag, or falling behind as technology rapidly develops, and underestimating the power of innovative tech can also be pitfalls for families, so staying informed about trends, getting expert advice, and being adaptable will be key for family offices moving forward.

One of the biggest questions moving forward is how AI might revolutionize the family office tech sector. Already, 81 percent of providers in Simple's 2023 survey are either currently using AI or plan to do so in the future.[6] From straightforward data extraction to complex portfolio analysis, its use can be extensive, and time will tell how it will continue to be integrated into the platforms and software used by family offices around the world.

> There are two types of family offices: those that have been hacked and those that don't realize they have been hacked.

Cybersecurity is increasingly on the minds of family office principals, and minimizing your exposure to risk is a crucial part of your family office technology concerns. The stats are pretty scary. I am of the belief that there are two types of family offices: those that have been hacked and those that don't realize they have been hacked. We are in the first camp, and still I wish our office took this area more seriously; some of the breaches we have had, while relatively minor, could have been avoided. Research on family offices often shows cybercrimes to be among the top five concerns of principals. The tools that hackers have are increasing in sophistication. People of wealth are relatively easy to detect—and are all targets. In my family alone, my sibling has been the victim of a professional-grade phishing email scam, and I have had my tax returns filed by a hacker hoping to intercept the refund payment. Recently, an RIA firm we work with shared that they had intercepted a sophisticated scam that would have misdirected a $7M wire payment for a vacation home for one of their clients.

This is happening frequently and is likely to increase. According to Eisner Amper, the following mistakes can leave a family office open to being hacked:[7]

- Not utilizing up-to-date user password and credentialing requirements, such as complex passwords and multifactor authentication

- Using outdated software without the latest security patches and antivirus updates

- Staff sharing access and user credentials (passwords) to an employee-issued device with family and friends, exposing the family office network

- Staff connecting an untested device such as a flash drive that could be a source of viruses and malware

- Sending unsecured emails

- Staff logging into public, insecure, or outdated Wi-Fi networks with office devices

Tom Boyden, cofounder and CEO of Legato Security and a former US intelligence officer, says, "To effectively reduce the risk and impact of cyber threats, family offices must adopt the mindset that they are just as much of a valid target for cyberattacks as enterprises, for two primary reasons: they hold very sensitive data on high-net-worth individuals that attackers can steal and hold for ransom, and attackers believe that family offices have deep pockets to pay out ransoms but generally have lax security practices and safeguards in place, making the task of stealing this information much easier than targeting a large enterprise with more sophisticated defenses. As such, family offices are typically perceived as the low-hanging fruit for attackers to monetize the data they seek to steal."

Despite all of these risks, many family offices don't take proper caution, especially smaller ones without the infrastructure that a larger one may have. Every family office will appreciate a cybersecurity specialist on the payroll. It need not be an in-house position if the office is on the smaller side, when a consultancy can work well. But there needs to be an ongoing annual investment in such services. Think of it as the same as proper accounting services or proper tax filing services: it is a must-have.

Such an expert will do an inventory of the office, understand all the players (family, nonfamily, in-house staff, service providers), prepare a risk assessment, and then suggest software and processes to help minimize risk. It is essential to have all individuals who have access to the family network on board. My middle and high school daughters undergo cybersecurity training appropriate for their age and computer usage at least twice a year.

The experts will help ensure that all endpoints (anything that connects to the network—phone, tablet, etc.) have the proper settings and software installed, can integrate with home A/V specialists to ensure home settings are appropriate as well, and will provide monitoring services for your network.

Ask your insurance broker about cybersecurity-specific coverage. Back up your critical information daily, so you cannot be held ransom. Use password managers, and follow all best practices you possibly can. It's a bit of money and it's a bit of a hassle, but it's nothing like what it costs to be hacked. Remember: Ojos abiertos. Keep your eyes open.

Family Office Costs

UBS says, "In this year's survey, the pure cost of operating a family office in 2022 was 38.1 basis points (bps) of asset under management."[8] Even modest family offices require a material financial investment, not to mention the investment in time and energy. Especially when there are multiple family lines in the family office, the costs can become a contentious issue. If the family office is located where only a subset of the family principals can utilize the space, it can cause friction and a desire to pare back what is seen as unnecessary costs. It is important that the principals don't fall into the trap of being penny wise and pound foolish, focusing too much on what may be unnecessary family office overhead and not appreciating the benefits and financial upside of the overall office for all members.

Family office costs can be broken down into five major categories: operating expenses, asset management costs, banking-related service fees, external structures, and other expenses. The first of these, the cost of running the office itself, is by far the largest chunk of total family office expenses and can be further broken down into staff costs, legal and compliance, infrastructure, tech, research, and other miscellaneous expenditures. However, many families expect tech and staff spending will increase moderately over the next three years.[9]

In speaking with many family offices, I've learned that many principals have only a fuzzy idea of the costs for a given provider or category of service (e.g., "legal") and, similarly, do not have a good handle on their overall costs, let alone how those compare with the costs of other offices. I have also seen situations where principals are unaware of the compensation structure of their providers, not knowing whether the provider charges on a time-and-materials basis, a fixed fee, AUM, or some other arrangement. It is crucial to understand the business model of all individuals and firms that provide services to the family office, and how this compares to the market rates.

The costs unsurprisingly vary widely based on your family office's size; a 2021 FORGE report showed that the average budget was $1.1M for an AUM of $250M or less, while for offices with more than $5B, the average was $20.8M.[10] The graphic below, pulled from the report, nicely demonstrates budgets as a function of AUM and how they are allocated:

Figure 7.2. Family Office Costs as % of Total

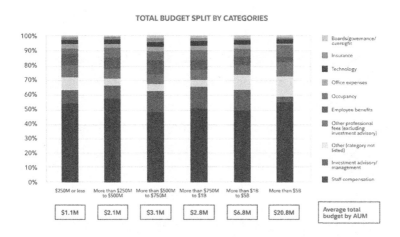

Source: Benchmarking Survey Report: Costs of Running a Family Office, FORGE Community, FMR LLC, 2021.

Total family office expenses also depend heavily on the nature and scale of the office itself. Portfolio characteristics can affect costs; offices that invest more heavily in private equity will need a larger share of staff with specialized expertise, for example. Size is a critical factor as well; for smaller offices of six employees, the costs will range from $1.5M to $1.8M per year, while larger-scale offices (over thirty employees) can be $14M to $22M.[11] However, while absolute expenses increase with larger offices, a higher AUM usually correlates with decreased operating costs as a fraction of AUM.

So how can family offices reduce expenses? First, investment fees can be hidden and difficult to discern, given the complexity of fee structures. In some cases, however, hidden fees can be tantamount to explicit fees.[12] Thorough benchmarking, research, negotiation, and monitoring industry trends can go a long way toward chipping away at some of these investment fees. Second, as we have seen, integrating tech into family office operations can be an effective way to enhance efficiency in onboarding, aggregation, portfolio analysis, and reporting. Last, outsourcing (or insourcing in certain scenarios) certain key functions—investment management, accounting, and tax preparation are all potential candidates—is another strategy for reducing costs but needs to be weighed along with the expertise required to do the job, the ability of the office to manage staff (or not), service levels, and so on. Ultimately, it is up to each individual office and their team to decide what makes sense for them given their goals, structure, size, and strategy.

WHAT WORKS

- Understanding the basics of accounting and how to read financial statements

- Analyzing what type of operational support the office requires and building a team of internal and external professionals to execute the work

WHAT DOESN'T

- Lacking cybersecurity protocols for each individual who is on your network

- Not understanding costs and the business model of each provider

CHAPTER 8

Investing Basics

Much like you must design a structure and leadership team to ensure that your family office will serve the specific needs of your family, you must implement your investing activities with the same thoughtfulness and planning. Investing is a fundamental part of the office; offices that perform poorly over time will not be sustainable no matter what else they may do well. It's crucial that you find the right professionals to work with, people with experience in the type of investments you'll focus on, and preferably a fiduciary experienced with family offices. However, in order to properly direct those professionals and to make informed decisions, a fundamental understanding of investing is an invaluable asset for every family principal.

At a basic level, there are six main asset classes that family offices and investors at large are concerned with: cash, public equity, fixed income, private equity, real assets, and hedge funds. Each of these classes has its own purpose, risks, and benefits. For example, having liquid cash on hand allows for flexibility, fee payments, and other expenses and as a backup against any losses from invested assets. There is not much risk to holding excess cash (aside from the opportunity cost), but depending on where it is housed, it may or may not generate material yields. You can generally hold your cash in money market funds or yield-bearing savings accounts to help keep up with inflation, and the fees will depend on the bank's structures and policies. Each of the other asset classes has its own advantages and disadvantages, as well as their own level of risk and reward.

To get a bird's-eye view, the average asset allocation in 2023 for family offices was as follows, according to a UBS report:[1]

Figure 8.1. Average Asset Allocation 2023

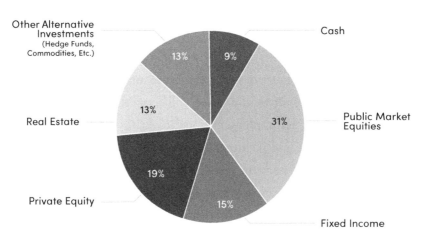

Source: UBS, Global Family Office Report 2023.

It is important that all of your family office principals have a sense of both how and why their portfolio is invested the way it is. The how involves the overall asset allocation, as well as how each class is invested. The why involves the rationale behind the overall allocation percentages (e.g., "Why do we have 65 percent of the investment portfolio in public equity?") and the rationale for any specific manager or investment (e.g., "Why did we choose State Street to manage the bond portfolio?"). Additionally, I've found it important that the principal understand how the performance and risk compare with benchmarks for both the overall portfolio and each asset class. The graphic below from Campden Wealth provides a bird's-eye view of family office allocation strategies for 2023.

Figure 8.2. Family Offices' Intention to Increase, Maintain, or Decrease Allocation to the Following Asset Classes in 2023

	Increase	Maintain	Decrease	Difference
Fixed Income — Developed Markets	13%	70%	17%	−4%
	18%	60%	22%	−4%
Fixed Income — Developing Markets	3%	86%	10%	−7%
	16%	68%	16%	0%
Equities — Developed Markets	24%	53%	23%	−1%
	36%	46%	18%	+18%
Equities — Developing Markets	14%	78%	8%	+6%
	26%	61%	13%	+13%
Private Equity — Direct Investments	41%	54%	5%	+36%
	41%	50%	9%	+32%
Private Equity — Funds	46%	45%	10%	+36%
	47%	44%	9%	+38%
Venture Capital	35%	55%	10%	+25%
	40%	50%	9%	+31%
Private Debt — Direct Lending	34%	59%	7%	+27%
	31%	61%	8%	+23%
Real Estate — Direct Investments	41%	47%	13%	+28%
	43%	43%	15%	+28%
REITS	8%	86%	6%	+2%
	13%	82%	5%	+8%
Hedge Funds	9%	76%	15%	−6%
	16%	71%	14%	+2%
Agriculture — (Forest, Farmland, Etc.)	18%	76%	5%	+13%
	23%	72%	6%	+17%
Commodities	22%	75%	4%	+18%
	31%	65%	4%	+27%
Gold, Precious Metals	8%	88%	5%	+3%
	18%	78%	4%	+14%
Cash or Cash Equivalent	20%	43%	37%	−17%
	20%	48%	31%	+11%
Cryptocurrency	24%	73%	3%	+21%
	26%	68%	5%	+21%
SPACs (Special Purpose Acquisition Company)	3%	89%	8%	−5%
	3%	87%	10%	−7%

North America   Global

Source: Campden Wealth, North America Family Office Report, 2022.

Risk

Even family office principals who have a high-level understanding of returns and asset classes tend to understand less well the concept of risk. Certainly, every investor intuitively understands that there is some risk in any investment, but understanding how to measure and balance risk in a portfolio is an important capability worth reviewing.

At the end of the day, risk means not having money when you need it, or even losing it completely; you can ride out greater volatility if you have enough liquid capital as a cushion. Furthermore, some asset classes are generally riskier than others; from least to most risky, the order is cash, fixed income, public equity, real estate, and private equity (particularly venture capital). Underappreciating the risk associated with your investments can be a disaster; there are no "unimportant risks with important assets," to paraphrase Morgan Housel in *The Psychology of Money.*

Generally speaking, the greater the return potential with an asset or investment class, the greater the risk of that asset or investment class. Public equity has a greater return potential (historically around 8–10 percent) than cash (which in recent years has been less than 1 percent). But what about risk? Using these two sample asset classes, does the risk profile tend to be around 10:1 to even things out? Sometimes. Another measure of risk is that of volatility, which, according to Investopedia, is "a statistical measure of the dispersion of returns for a given security or market index."[2] For fixed income (based on the US treasury index), volatility is typically between roughly 3 and 7 percent, and public equity sits at 10–20 percent, as measured by the S&P 500.[3] There are additional measures of risk, including standard deviation, beta, and others. For me, what has worked is zeroing in on one measure and then reporting on that alongside return and benchmark data. If you are not tracking risk currently, in my view it is a must-have to add it to the list.

It is important that investors understand what level of risk their portfolio is operating at and how that level compares with liquidity needs and performance goals of the portfolio. At times, money managers may take outsized risk on a portfolio in order to seek returns, and if this is done, the capital owner needs to be aware of it and comfortable with that risk.

Benchmarking

Benchmarking both the returns and the risk of a portfolio—in aggregate and by asset class—is required to understand the performance of a portfolio. Benchmarking is comparing a certain metric—say, whether your investment has risen in value—with other investments in the market or with general trends. It is a crucial step in understanding how well your investments are doing in context.

When a chief investment officer or financial manager says, "We were up 17 percent last year" or that "the emerging market portfolio had a -3 percent performance last quarter," the first question to ask is, "Compared to what?" If the overall portfolio was up 17 percent but the benchmark was up 22 percent, I am not a happy investor. Similarly, if my emerging market portion was down 3 percent, but the relevant benchmark was down 13 percent, I would feel pretty good.

When benchmarking your overall portfolio, it is important to not change the benchmarks unless there is an obvious reason to do so, which will enable you to have a better sense of how things are going over multiple time periods—ideally multiple years. It is also important to benchmark both the manager's recommended asset allocation and their fund selection.

Benchmarking liquid asset classes such as cash, public debt, and public equity is easier than benchmarking private assets, especially private equity funds, which tends to require at least five years of data before any meaningful assessment might be made. For some private equity and venture capital funds, the last few years of the fund life may provide the bulk of the returns and, therefore, the performance data. Private direct investments may start to show meaningful performance signs after two to three years, but some require more time.

Don't let those time frames concern you. Family office investors tend to take the long-term view with investing performance, especially if there are younger generations that may not have an immediate need for the assets for ten or more years.

WHAT WORKS

- Recognizing what your knowledge gap is with respect with what you know today and what you need to know to effectively manage the managers

- Continually growing your financial management skills via conferences, webcasts, networking, reading

WHAT DOESN'T

- Not tracking and not understanding risk of both the office's asset allocation and of each manager and fund across the portfolio

- Cherry-picking your benchmarking or performance; be sure to look at all assets over the proper amount of time to get a true picture of performance

CHAPTER 9

Asset Classes

There are a variety of common asset classes that are effective vehicles for family office investment. As such, it's important to choose the classes that best suit your family office's tolerance for risk and desire for returns, the need for cash flow, and tax implications. Understanding each of these can help you make the best decision—and to evaluate the recommendations of your investment managers—for your specific situation.

Public Equity and Fixed Income

For many family offices, public equity and fixed income are where the lion's share of their portfolio resides. These were traditionally called stocks and bonds, but are now often referred to as public equity and fixed income.

With fixed income, as the name suggests, the primary goal is often to generate stable, dependable income year over year. Bonds are also used to protect against the volatility of equities and as a source of diversification. The main risks here include increases in inflation suppressing the value of your yields and the bond issuer defaulting. High-yield bonds, some corporate bonds, and junk bonds are the riskiest in this asset class, whereas US Treasuries are seen as relatively low risk. Government-issued bonds are generally tax deductible, providing further incentives for investment in them.

Public equity is among one of the biggest categories of investment. BlackRock's 2022 family office survey showed that, globally, family office allocations for public equity came to 37 percent.[1]

The main goal with equities is typically growth or income, or achieving a happy medium between the two.

"The primary purpose of public equities in the family's portfolio," a family office principal with deep expertise in public market investing tells us, "is to capture the equity risk premium. The family ought to own broad market exposure so that they can benefit from the general drift higher in equities." The particular securities and funds selected will reflect a family's preferred strategies. There is a broad range of risk levels and associated returns with public equities, so your family's approach will depend on your appetite and tolerance for risk.

For public equities, the top sector preferences among family offices as of 2023 include technology, health care, and energy.[2] In 2021, family offices achieved 17 percent and 10 percent public equity returns in developed and developing markets, respectively.[3]

The fees for public equity and fixed income vary across funds and management strategies, including expense ratios; sales loads; brokerage commission; transaction, exchange, redemption, and 12b-1 fees. Clearly, there are many ways your capital may be subject to different charges, so it is important to clearly read and understand fund prospectuses and fee structures, particularly given that these charges can build up over time and detract quite significantly from your earnings.

Another consideration is whether your capital will be invested via a basket of individually picked securities or whether you should hire an outside manager to create a separately managed account (SMA) on your family's behalf. There is also the decision around active versus passive investment strategies. The active approach is generally more costly than passive managed portfolios, where you might invest into an index (e.g., the S&P 500 or the NASDAQ). Active managers may charge in the 100 bps range or more, and while there are many asset allocators that are of the mind that active management can deliver enough additional returns over the course of several years to cover for these relatively high fees, there are many who don't believe in the concept of active management in the public markets.

As always, for any family office, the allocation choices will depend on the individual office's goals, capacity, risk tolerance and appetite, expertise, and time horizons.

Private Equity

Private equity refers to investments made in private companies that are not listed on a public stock exchange. As such, they carry more risk and are therefore generally only available to institutional and accredited investors such as family offices. Private equity operators generally have more flexibility than those in public companies because they do not have the pressure of quarterly earnings and can take a more long-term, strategic approach to value creation. The general goal for private equity firms is to acquire companies and enhance their value via growth plans, efficiency increases, cost cuts, or management changes, and to make a profit when they either sell the company to a buyer or via an initial public offering.

Private equity provides another source of diversification, as well as an avenue to outsized returns, according to Ryan Harris, a partner at Kirkland & Ellis LLP, a leader of a private investment and family office practice. "When you look at the performance data," Harris says, "they are pretty consistent, net of fees, and they don't typically have the volatility of the public markets."

Family offices can participate via direct deals or through funds that generally last seven to ten years. As of mid-2022, private equity assets under management was $7.6 trillion globally.[4] According to a 2023 UBS family office survey, family offices allocated on average 19 percent of their portfolios to this asset class (10 percent funds or funds of funds, 9 percent direct investments).[5] For direct investments, top sectors include technology, real estate, health care, and consumer goods.[6]

The private equity landscape can shift dramatically in a short period of time. For example, there has been a major shift in private equity investing since 2021 due to rising inflation and interest rates, geopolitical instability, and economic uncertainty and volatility. As of mid-2023, depressed deal flow has led to $3.9 trillion in dry powder (unallocated capital) among private equity firms. Additionally, in 2023, global buyout exit value declined by 66 percent and deal value by 60 percent compared to their peaks in 2021.[7]

In terms of fees, private equity typically follows a 2 and 20 structure, with management fees around 2 percent annually and performance fees (typically in the form of carried interest) hovering at about 20 percent, often when returns exceed a certain threshold known as the "hurdle rate."

Venture Capital

Venture capital is a subset of private equity that focuses on start-ups and early-stage companies and is the riskiest form of private equity. As a subset of the broader alternative investments asset class, venture capital enables investors to direct funds toward start-ups and other companies in the early stages of growth. According to a 2022–2023 BlackRock study, 47 percent of the 120 single family offices surveyed invest in venture capital,[8] with allocation of 6 percent globally, per a 2022 Campden Wealth survey.[9] The total capital raised by venture capital is projected to be $468.4 billion in

2024,[10] and while the sector is highly risky (90 percent of start-ups fail), when it is successful, it can yield returns that vastly outperform public markets.[11] Keep in mind, the top quartile of venture capital fund managers tend to significantly outperform the rest of the market; getting access into top funds is paramount in terms of returns.

For many family offices, venture capital can be a means of reaching diversification, liquidity, and higher returns. For many families, highly entrepreneurial companies were the original source of their wealth, so they may have the knowledge, expertise, and confidence to allocate substantial capital to the venture capital ecosystem due to their own experience building wealth. Finally, venture capital can provide ample opportunities to generate positive change in a family's

> The top quartile of venture capital fund managers tend to significantly outperform the rest of the market; getting access into top funds is paramount in terms of returns.

sector of interest, given the ability to invest directly into a solution to a problem or cause that you care deeply about such as climate change or cancer therapies. In this sense, it can be closely intertwined with impact investing for the family office.

Just as motivations vary, so too do the approaches families take to venture capital: direct investment, funds, or funds of funds. Competition for direct deals is intense, and access can be difficult, but this is where family office networks and collaboration can come in handy. Family offices are often able to leverage relationships with money managers to get into the most sought-after venture capital funds, those with proven track records and many successful exits in their portfolio. These managed funds can be costly in terms of fees, but access is much easier, and it does help reduce the substantial risk of venture capital investing. As of March 2023, some of the most prominent industries in venture capital among family offices include health care, blockchain, gaming, space, and climate tech.[12]

In terms of performance and market prospects, analysis from Cambridge Associates showed that venture capital private index median performance stood at 15.5 percent over a fifteen-year period ending in 2020, with the top active managers achieving rates of over 45 percent and the worst performers incurring losses.[13] The choice of manager when exploring the venture capital space is therefore quite important.

Figure 9.1. Average Annual Manager Returns by Asset Class 1/1/06 – 12/31/20

	Core/Core + Bonds	EM	US LC Value	Global ex US Eq	US SC Value	US LC Growth	US SC Growth	Hedge Funds	Global RE	Global PE	Global VC
n	147	43	201	130	131	163	102	250	770	1,179	1,031
5th %ile	6.7%	10.5%	10.9%	8.8%	11.7%	15.3%	16.8%	12.6%	24.7%	36.9%	49.7%
Median	5.2%	8.1%	8.5%	5.9%	8.8%	12.0%	12.6%	6.7%	9.3%	13.3%	15.5%
Dispersion	1.5%	2.4%	2.4%	2.9%	2.9%	3.3%	4.2%	5.9%	15.4%	23.6%	34.2%

Source: Building Winning Portfolios Through Private Investments, Cambridge Associates LLC, Aug 2021.

Josh Cohen, founder and managing partner at City Light Capital and cofounder of The ImPact and Impact Capital Managers, says that family offices generally invest "around 2–5 percent" in venture capital. "In some cases, [that is] as high as 10 percent. Keep in mind that [venture capital] as a class may lead to significant appreciation, but there is a long duration on the capital—typically ten to twelve years before you get it back. As such, venture capital is often a strong fit for the next generation, family foundations, and trusts that take a long-term approach to investing and that can have any cash needs met by other means.

"Even with impact venture capital funds, most managers attempt to generate or exceed market rates for the asset class," Cohen continues. "For example, in the Impact Capital Managers network, the overwhelming majority of the 120 members are targeting market rate returns." But there are nonfinancial benefits as well: "It can be an excellent way to learn about business building from the ground floor. It can be incredibly rewarding to be part of turning nothing into something."

Your Own Firm

Many family offices get excited about private equity and venture capital to the point that they desire to set up their own internal shop. This can go well, or not. Many family offices that do try to bring this type of investing internally find that it takes more time and money than they originally envisioned.

Competition for strong private equity investors is fierce among family offices. Ryan Harris says, "A family office evaluating building from scratch a private equity team needs to understand that there is a material cost to attracting and keeping the kind of talent required to operate the fund, and this talent is in short supply these days."

Generating deal flow, finding the time and expertise to properly apply due diligence to candidate companies, and even the operational element of the private equity investing can prove more challenging than expected. Some family offices give it a shot and then back out and resort to investing via funds. It's a good idea to be fully aware when setting up internal operations that you are making a commitment of time, money, and other resources for at least an eight- to ten-year period.

Real Estate

BlackRock's 2022–2023 global single family office survey[14] found that 63 percent of families invested in real estate, with the portfolio allocations of 13 percent in 2022, according to a UBS study.[15] This asset class can offer several benefits to investors, such as long-term growth, diversification, and risk mitigation. Family offices, specifically, can take advantage of exclusive opportunities via networks, partnerships, and relationships in the industry, and some offices for whom this sector was the original source of their wealth are more comfortable allocating most of their assets to real estate. However, it is also an industry that requires highly localized investment knowledge and expertise. Other potential risks and challenges include illiquidity and volatility in interest rates, inflation, employment, and so on. However, through due diligence, research, and alignment of strategy with goals, families can use real estate investments to their benefit and generate long-term growth that can persist across generations.

Real estate consists of both traditional and nontraditional subclasses. The traditional categories include residential, commercial, industrial, and undeveloped land, and the nontraditional subclass includes low income housing, data centers, health care offices, medical facilities, and assisted living.[16] According to Smartland, as of 2022, the most common real estate sectors for family office investment in North America include residential homes and multifamily apartments (88%), offices (56%), and industrial or logistics complexes (46%), with retail (35%) and hotels (29%) lagging in popularity.[17]

Performance in this sector varies by segment; in some areas such as commercial real estate, interest rate hikes and sluggish demand have heightened difficulties for investors, yet prospects remain more optimistic for segments like logistics, student housing, and senior living.[18] Simple & Co. highlights that nontraditional subclasses have grown in popularity among family offices due to forces such as demographics, infrastructure development, globalization, innovation, and technology.[19] Macroeconomic trends will affect each subclass differently; for example, supply chain trends will have different impacts on retailers' and logistics companies' profits and lease payments.

In 2023, 55 percent and 26 percent of SFO investors surveyed by BlackRock planned to maintain or increase their allocations in real estate, respectively.[20] In response to market volatility, high inflation, rising interest rates, and diminished central bank liquidity, families began to revisit their alternative allocations at large in order to reposition themselves in this changing environment.

For family offices starting in real estate, Mazyar Mortazavi, CEO of TAS Impact, recommends "starting by identifying the right managers that align with the investment objectives of the family. Given the breadth of real estate investment opportunities, a family may choose several managers with focused experience to align with the investment objectives of the portfolio . . . The value of a multimanager approach is the access to a diverse set of deals and also the opportunity to garner multiple perspectives. Creating that internally requires a significant investment and scale of team to achieve a similar outcome. An internal team is most effective if the family wants to focus in a specific area of real estate and can identify a team lead who comes in with a partner frame of mind."

WHAT WORKS

- Awareness of the return expectations, risk levels, and illiquidity characteristics of each asset class

WHAT DOESN'T

- Thinking it will be easy to find talent to run an internal PE or VC arm of the family office; professionals are in short supply and are highly compensated by institutional players

- Not understanding fee structures and how they compare with other providers and options (e.g., active management), and the value add vis-à-vis performance

CHAPTER 10

Sustainable and Impact Investing

Beyond individual asset classes, family offices are increasingly investing in a way that is aligned with their values. Sustainable investing, which we will use here as the umbrella term that also includes impact investing and environmental, social, and corporate governance (ESG) investing, is a way to invest—in any asset class and in any sector—where the goal is to both have a financial return and to create positive social or environmental impact. What differs between sustainable and traditional investing is that the goal to create a social or environmental impact alongside the financial return is intentional and measurable.

Mazyar Mortazavi argues that businesses—including family offices—should invest in a way that includes "financial, social, cultural, and environmental capital. Once we calculate all of these, we get to the net effective cost [and] return of the investments that we make." His company, TAS Impact (which focuses on real estate development but with the explicit purpose of creating a positive impact for society), has shown this to be a financially viable path that also generates a positive impact on the world. "We take the view that we are generational stewards. This informs how we make decisions today with a lens to the future."

Making an impact from philanthropy is very common among family offices, while leveraging the for-profit sector via investing is a newer concept for many.

Justin Rockefeller, principal of the Rockefeller family office, believes that impact investing is another way to solve problems, and if you limit the options to just philanthropy, you are not using all the tools in your tool belt. "We need all shots on goal to address some of the most pressing challenges to people and planet," he says. "Let's not limit the potential solutions."

Sustainable investing, in the majority of cases, has the intention of achieving market rate returns on top of some wider impact. A minority of sustainable investments are designed to be impact first and achieve concessionary returns, meaning that they create impact as the primary goal and also achieve a financial return which may be lower than the prevailing market returns.

Justin tells us that sustainable investments are most sought after by women, millennials, and some Gen Z principals. Many younger family office principals are keen to explore sustainable investing, and this is a key way for the older generation in the family office to engage with the younger generation. According to Morgan Stanley, in 2021, 99 percent of millennials indicated they were interested in sustainable investing (57 percent very interested), compared with 79 percent of the general population (41 percent very interested).[1]

Over the last decade, sustainable investing has increased dramatically across the globe, both in the public markets, where it is typically referred to as sustainable investing or ESG investing, and in the private markets, where it is typically referred to as impact investing. In the public markets, investors may take the first step to actively remove investments, funds, or managers that invest in categories that don't align with the investor. For example, companies that manufacture military weapons, or media and technology companies that support pornography, or companies that run for-profit prisons are removed from a portfolio. This is called negative screening, and the offending investments are often called sin stocks. The investor doesn't want to support businesses or industries that they believe are creating harm in the world, and as such redirects their capital into other investments.

From there, many investors will then seek companies that score high on ESG ratings; these companies attempt to benefit all stakeholders in their work, not solely their shareholders. A good example would be Microsoft Corporation. The company does not have as its principal mission to help the environment or underserved communities, yet it scores high on a wide variety of environmental, social, and governance measures. Some investors choose to support such companies, rather than not, as a way to increase their investment's social impact; other investors believe that high-scoring ESG companies also perform better (higher returns and/or lower risk) than peer companies that don't score as high on ESG measures. Public debt (bonds and credit) also allows sustainable investors to find options, such as municipal bonds and other projects for underserved communities (public housing, education in low-income districts, etc.).

A third dimension of sustainable investing is direct (or indirect via impact funds) investing into for-profit social impact companies. These companies are designed from their inception to create solutions to specific problems, and they are typically referred to as impact investments. Examples include for-profit financial services companies that have a mission to serve underrepresented populations such as immigrants, people of color, or ethnic minorities. It can include companies targeting a healthier environment, such as those that capture excess methane from oil-drilling rigs.

Around the same time I took more of a leadership position in my family office, I was first learning about sustainable and impact investments. I was struck by the power of the core idea that for-profit companies can leverage their business model to simultaneously create financial returns and social impact. Like all family offices, ours was making plenty of financial investments (without knowledge or regard to any impact we may be creating via our investments), and we were also active givers to philanthropic causes. We treated these as two separate activities, with no overlap. The concept of sustainable investing was fairly mind bending for me at the time. I knew intuitively that all companies have positive and negative side effects, beyond what the core purpose of that company may be . . . yet I never gave thought to the idea that the entire purpose of a company could be to solve a social or environmental problem, and further that one could find and invest in such companies. This aha moment reframed how I looked at investing in general . . . from a somewhat mundane activity that was not core to my chosen profession, to one that had the power to create value for the broader society, while also achieving returns—a win-win. As another method to create positive change in addition to philanthropy and grant making, investing into for-profit companies suddenly became something I needed to explore. (To avoid confusion, while you can invest in not-for-profit entities, for the purposes of this discussion, we can think of investing as only for for-profit entities and philanthropy only for not-for-profit entities, but know that it can get even more nuanced if you want to dig further.)

Another reason sustainable and impact investing resonated with me was my children. Every parent I have ever spoken with has said that the process of becoming a parent has changed their worldview in a pretty dramatic way. In my case, it was shifting who I felt accountable to, from my parents to my children. Prior to kids, I felt a great deal of accountability to do right by my parents, to make them proud, and to care for the family wealth properly and to be a good steward of it. Soon after the dust settled and I had my second child, I started to think deeply about the world in which they would live, well past my time. I realized that I had the strong desire to do right by my kids as well, and part of that was helping to influence the world my children would inherit. Sustainable investing resonated with me since I realized I had capital, and I had great latitude on how it could be deployed. I could seek out returns while also making a positive impact in some way, and that became the primary way I wanted to think about deploying capital from that point forward.

As a capital owner, I don't believe I or anyone else has a responsibility to pursue things such as impact investing, yet I do think all capital owners—no matter what size the capital base—have a responsibility to think about how their capital is making a difference, as well as how it could make a difference in the world, depending on how it is invested. And in the case of sustainable investing, it's more than a responsibility; it's an opportunity. If we think about climate change and the opportunity to invest in battery platforms, for example, I believe there are huge financial opportunities to be had that will also benefit society.

> Sustainable investing is more than a responsibility; it's an opportunity.

I was keen to learn more and started to have conversations with the financial manager at the family office about the topic. What I find over and over is many family office principals who try to inquire with their manager on the topic get a cold reception. Still to this day, what I recommend to family office principals who want to learn more about the possibilities is to do research in addition to what your manager may send your way. There are many networks and professional groups where one can learn about sustainable investing and find plenty of investment opportunities (see appendix D that lists networks).

My geography was my asset for jumping into the sustainable investing pool. Northern California is ground zero for start-ups and early-stage investing, and I began making a small number of investments into early-stage for-profit social enterprises. This aligned with the services business I had created around this same period to provide training, education, and consulting to CEOs and investors in the social impact ecosystem; it was synergistic. Fast-forward to 2024, and we have created a portfolio of over thirty investments across many sectors—education technology, digital health, sustainable food, sustainable energy, and economic opportunity. Working with and supporting these CEOs—incredibly talented and passionate leaders—has given me and my colleague Angie such incredible joy. We feel privileged to support talented visionaries who are committed to their cause like no other entrepreneurs I have ever known. Financially speaking, the fund is performing on par with other early-stage VC funds, and I am proud to be backing companies working every day to address a social or environmental problem.

A couple of years ago, I had the opportunity to bring my daughters to one of the demo days that my company produced. Demo days are where early-stage companies will present their work, typically a five-minute pitch to potential investors. In part due to the fact that social enterprise start-ups tend to be more gender balanced than typical tech start-ups (our portfolio is approximately balanced 50/50; the average representation of women in general tech CEOs is a dismal low single-digit percentage), my girls were blown away.

"Dad…that was really cool seeing these girls on stage talking about their start-ups," my older one told me.

I have been able to parlay my daughter's interest in start-ups into a broader discussion on investing. I think, for a brief second, that my daughter actually thought I was somewhat cool for the work I was doing! More importantly, it was a way to expose her to a part of the family office that she could relate to. And I have seen time and again how the next generation resonates with not only socially responsible investing but also with early-stage entrepreneurship. I am so excited to have found a way to combine both in our family office, and I believe it will continue to catch the interest of my children.

Although the younger principals support impact investing in concept, in many cases, they have to lobby their elders to move capital. The older generation is concerned that they can't make real returns, that impact investing is a fad, or maybe that there are not enough opportunities. These hesitant investors, according to Veris Wealth Partners CEO Stephanie Cohn Rupp, may "lack education on the fundamental and existential risks posed by climate change. It is unfortunate, as they are continuing to fuel an obsolete economic model that is harmful to people and planet and climate and is also a material financial risk. Sustainable investing is basically better investing taking into account more variables."

And it may be better investing when you look just at the financial numbers, too. Organizations such as GIIN reported the size of the sustainable investment industry at $1.164 trillion as of December 2021.[2] The data shows that ESG investing is also good financial investing: Kroll's ESG and Global Investor Returns study showed that, from 2013 to 2021, public equity funds of companies with the best MSCI ESG ratings outperformed the funds of lower-rated companies.[3] The global leaders (those with ratings of AAA–AA) achieved a compound annual return of 12.9 percent; those rated B–CCC were around 8.6 percent.

Impact investing is generally achieved via direct investments and impact funds investing into private companies that are building solutions to social or environmental problems. The Impact Capital Managers association, a community of impact venture capital funds, has over 120 funds, the majority of which are targeting market rate returns. Research has shown that such impact funds can achieve lower rates of risk than those funds not focused on impact.[4]

Stephanie Cohn Rupp recommends that family offices "hire consultants to explain the approach of sustainable finance" or hire "professionals who have ESG experience. Recruiting a senior director of research with ESG experience can immediately help educate the family office on the terminology, analysis, networks, and events in this space." The core of this approach is that the family office's leadership must embrace the focus on sustainable investment. "If there is no buy-in from the leadership," Stephanie continues, "the family office will waste time and remain unable to develop a point of view on sustainable investing options. The issue here is truly about consensus building. If there is consensus to invest this way, the roadblocks become minimal."

Donor-advised funds (DAF) are another place to start, says Jed Emerson, chief impact officer at AlTi Tiedemann Global. "A subset of DAF administrators (Impact Assets is one in particular) makes it relatively easy to deploy one's capital into a for-profit socially impactful company or fund," Jed says. "The interesting thing here is that any returns that accrue from the investment go back into the DAF and may be used for future donations or impact investments. Additionally, a family office may decide to create an investment sleeve to focus on sustainable and impact investments" such as venture funds focused on ESG start-ups.

Jed has also seen how some family offices have found that involving the next generation in impact investing is a great mechanism to provide that younger generation exposure to the family office. Younger principals tend to relate to the entrepreneurs with a social mission, both in age and values alignment. Jed says of one of his firm's client families, "The older generation stated pretty clearly they didn't want to explore sustainable investing options." But the father was open to his daughter's strong feelings about making a difference in animal welfare. The advisor suggested that they invest in "companies with good track records with respect to animal welfare, and not . . . in companies with poor records." That convinced the patriarch and "also helped engage the next generation in the family office strategic planning and operations." Impact investing can provide a great learning opportunity and motivation for the next generation while opening a new avenue for the elder principals to similarly rethink how to best utilize their capital base.

Sustainable Investing in the Real World

A variety of factors indicate, at least on the surface, that family offices are the perfect type of entities to make sustainable and impact investments, including their long time horizon, active participation in private funds and direct investing already, and multiple pools of capital from which to invest. Any fund manager or social entrepreneur will have an easy time raising capital from family offices, right? Well, let's dig into the reality of how family offices are participating in sustainable capital today.

> 56 percent of the family offices have sustainable investments.

From the UBS Global Family Office Report 2022, we see that roughly 56 percent of the family offices have sustainable investments. Of those that do, the most common technique is negative screening; the common industries that investors choose to eliminate from their portfolios are typically those fossil fuel, tobacco, and weapons manufacturing companies. This aggregate figure is broken down in a surprising way: for US-based family offices, it is 39 percent, while in Western Europe, the Middle East, Africa, and Latin America, it is between 60 and 70 percent.[5]

Digging a bit deeper, approximately 31 percent of family offices support ESG in the public markets, and about 24 percent make impact investments.

There are a couple of different ways to read this data.

On one hand, it could be said that sustainable investing has become a quite common practice, in one form or another. If we went back just one decade, it would certainly be much rarer to see family offices participating in sustainable investing, in any of its forms. Technically speaking, the practice is seen in the majority of the family offices.

On the other hand, having some sustainable investments and supporting the practice in a material way may be two very different things. For some sustainable investors, deploying negative screens on public market investing is table stakes; it may be the case that a family office has less than 1 percent of its capital deployed to sustainable investing to be counted in the 56 percent figure. Even the 24 percent of family offices that have some impact investments may be a rounding error in terms of the total capital the family office has to deploy. It's likely safe to assume that of the 25 percent that make impact investments, only a subset (perhaps 8 percent of total) have material impact investment holdings. Still, if that means 10 percent of all family offices are material impact investors, that can represent a large amount of capital. And it also means there is much, much more capital that could be deployed in the coming years.

Of those family offices that still don't invest sustainably, 27 percent point to lack of standard definitions of sustainability as a barrier to investing.[6] In interviews, several family office principals also pointed to investment managers who know little about impact investing, lack of deal flow, and finally many who believe the family office already supports social impact initiatives via its philanthropy. To be clear on this last point, it is less likely they believe their family foundation or DAF investing the endowment sustainably, rather it is more likely they believe their grants to not-for-profits are a sufficient means of supporting social and environmental initiatives.

As for the returns from sustainable investing, it is challenging to make sweeping statements, given it covers many different asset classes, many geographies, and importantly, a wide variety of goals on the part of the investor; the Global Impact Investing Network data shows that approximately two-thirds of impact investments, in terms of the expectations of the investor, are market rate and not concessionary.[7]

Drew Payne is CEO of UpMetrics, which provides services to impact investors, as well as a principal in his own family office. He submits that a number of factors are considered in addition to financial return. "From an investment point of view, we look at a variety of core elements. That includes diversification, tax and cash flow planning, and expectation for benchmark or higher returns."

Family offices historically list the ability to achieve market-based returns as a concern and reason for not participating, but this seems to be changing fairly quickly. Now, as many as 80 percent of family offices believe sustainable investments will continue to at least match broader market returns over the next five years. Except for the US family offices, which are more pessimistic about returns, this trend is consistent in other parts of the world.

Sustainable investing is certainly gaining ground as attitudes shift; according to UBS, family offices anticipate that ESG-integration investments will constitute about a quarter of all portfolios (24%) with negative screening accounting for 30% and impact investing at 14%.[8] Concerns remain as to how to best measure impact, but the field of SI is gathering momentum and there are ample opportunities to become involved.

WHAT WORKS

- Aligning the full capital stack of the family office to its mission and values, realizing the impact is achieved via investments, not solely philanthropy

- Utilizing sustainable and impact investing as a way to engage the next generations into the family business

- Leveraging beyond-the-dollar support in addition to capital; for-profit start-ups with social missions need knowledge, connections, and mentoring

WHAT DOESN'T

- Avoiding sustainable investing due to the false assumption that it leads to concessionary returns; doing so will cause the family to miss out on many good investments

- Assuming that all sustainable investments have high impact; most do, but some do not meet their sustainability goals

CHAPTER 11

Philanthropy

I have yet to come across a family office that is not engaged in philanthropy, and in most cases, such families are donating significant amounts of capital. Indeed, for many family office principals, this is the most enjoyable part of their work. Whether they are giving directly from family funds, establishing a family foundation, or giving via a donor-advised fund (DAF), the activity of making charitable gifts to help the broader society is one that families appreciate and often bond over.

Many families are giving from a pooled family entity (a fund or a foundation) and often principals choose to donate additionally to their own set of grantees from their own sources of capital. Many family principals have the opportunity to serve on the board of the foundations and grantees they give to and, in this way, can also share their expertise and leverage their network.

In the cases where a family foundation may exist, the endowment of the foundation may also be a source of increasing the family's impact. The funds need not (and perhaps should not) be invested traditionally like other commercial investments until they are given away. Rather, as the endowment funds are already designated as philanthropic capital, they may be invested in sustainable strategies and funds until they are given to grantees. This is an often overlooked way a family can increase its impact and also begin to invest sustainably in addition to doing so in the main investment portfolios of the family.

Justin Rockefeller believes that philanthropists should give to causes that have no obvious market-based solutions, that are important, tractable, neglected, and, ideally after those criteria are met, for which the donor also has a personal or institutional connection or passion. Given the sense of special obligation he and some of his relatives feel to mitigating climate change because of their ancestors' historical ties to the fossil fuel industry, and because of the enormity of the challenge, he both invests in for-profit companies and donates to NGOs addressing it. Capital allocators can tackle pressing social or environmental challenges using multiple tools on their tool belts, including of course capital through investing and philanthropy, but also using time, network, expertise, influence, passion, voice, and vote.

In 2022, family donations amounted to $11M on average globally according to Campden Wealth. Some of the most popular causes included education, economic and social impact, health care, environment, political and civil issues, and conflict and peace.[1] Data for high-net-worth giving broken down by wealth and income levels is scarce, but a 2021 article published in the *National Tax Journal* provided the statistics that follow. It was calculated using 2016 IRS data.

Table 11.1. Higher-Income Giving (IRS Statistics of Income)

IRS SOI INCOME GROUPS	PERCENTAGE GIVING > 0	MEAN AMOUNT GIVEN ($)	MEAN PERCENTAGE OF INCOME GIVEN
$200,000–$500,000	85.2	6,302	1.97
$500,000–$1,000,000	88.5	16,831	2.32
$1,000,000–$1,500,000	86.4	36,088	2.78
$1,500,000–$2,000,000	86.8	53,300	2.91
$2,000,000–$5,000,000	88.3	108,119	3.44
$5,000,000–$10,000,000	92.2	308,269	4.32
$10,000,000+	94.6	2,661,195	8.57

Note: 2016 IRS Statistics of Income (SOI) tables report the number of filers in each income group as well as the number of itemizers. Means in this table are calculated assuming that nonitemizers do not make any donations.

Source: Jonathan Meer and Benjamin A. Priday, "Generosity Across the Income and Wealth Distributions," *National Tax Journal,* Volume 74, No. 3, September 2021.

Campden Wealth's North America Family Office Report 2022 broke down the major avenues for charitable giving and the percentage of family offices in the study that utilized each. Most gave through their family foundation, followed by direct donations to a cause of choice, then to a specific charity of choice.

In terms of a question many new donors face—whether to set up a traditional family foundation or instead give via a donor-advised fund—Catherine Crystal Foster of Rockefeller Philanthropy Advisors says of foundations and donor-advised funds, "Many people with a foundation also have a DAF, but the reverse is certainly not true. For some, the DAF is an experimental place for the younger generation or a spouse" to invest in a cause "that may not be aligned with the family foundation if there is one in place . . . With a foundation, one can exert control in some ways that you can't in a DAF; however, it's not accurate to think that within a DAF, the donor doesn't have meaningful control. The other structure you see at times is the LLC—which allows for investments into for-profit socially impactful entities yet does not provide the tax deductibility when funds are transferred into the LLC." Another reason some choose to utilize the LLC structure is that it allows for privacy.

Figure 11.1. Vehicles Used by the Family in Support of Philanthropic Giving

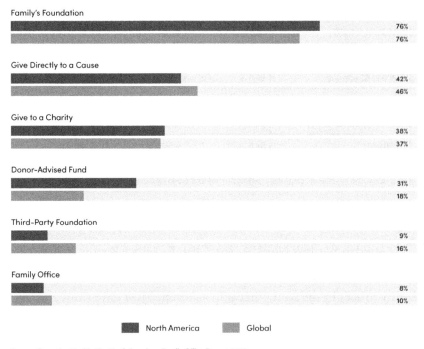

Source: Campden Wealth, The North American Family Office Report, 2023.

Philanthropy is typically triggered at various stages of a family office. Catherine says, "Typical catalysts may be the passing of a family member or the sale of a family business." She goes on to say that younger people are giving more than they did in the past.

"We are seeing more of the spend-down philosophy at work, donors feeling like they want to make a larger impact, and do so during their lifetime." Other recent trends in philanthropy include offering general operating support for nonprofits (as opposed to restricted project support) and sustainable investing with the endowment capital of a foundation.

There are also innovative ways that families are blending traditional philanthropy and commercial investing to make a positive impact. Indeed, the lines can be quite blurry. While most family offices traditionally separate out investing and philanthropy, Gary and Laura Lauder have identified a more nuanced approach, which in turn allows them to create more social impact in their work alongside their traditional investing. They have identified and deployed capital into four buckets:

1. **Finance Only** for traditional investing

2. **Finance First, Impact Second** (e.g., investments into clean energy funds or direct investments)

3. **Social First, Finance Second** (e.g., recoverable grants that recycle the capital into future social causes)

4. **Social Only**, which includes grant making to not-for-profits and other charitable entities, with no financial return

According to the Lauders, this approach enables them to activate a much larger proportion of their capital base and dramatically scale the impact they achieve. In their words, "While we still invest in buckets one and four, increasingly, it's the investments in buckets two and three that provide the prospects for massive scale. Since we are all looking for the most impactful and scalable models, investments in buckets two and three have the most potential!"[2]

In this way, a family office need not limit their impact to philanthropic

> A typical family office might be able to leverage 20, 50, or 100 times the amount of capital toward a social cause as compared to only utilizing philanthropic dollars.

grants. They can use commercial investments, which are typically a significant multiple of their philanthropic dollars, and invest them sustainably. A typical family office might be able to leverage 20, 50, or 100 times the amount of capital toward a social cause as compared to only utilizing philanthropy dollars.

My own family foundation has been a great vehicle to make donations to local not-for-profit entities that we, as a family, care about and are connected to, and we invest the endowment as sustainably as possible. There are countless examples of families in which the most collaborative and fun work of the family office is determining the mission for family philanthropy, identifying and choosing grantees, and working in other beyond-the-dollar ways of giving time, expertise, and connections to drive impact. And the greater the collaboration and integration there is among the family principals, the greater the involvement with other family office topics and activities, all leading to increased family office effectiveness and sustainability.

WHAT WORKS

- Aligning philanthropy with the family office mission and values, and as a powerful convening tool for family members to jointly plan and grant funds

- Utilizing the endowment to make sustainable and impact investments

- Principals leveraging their expertise and networks with socially aligned investments and grantees of the family office

WHAT DOESN'T

- Not having a strategy for giving or blindly setting up a foundation, thinking it will best meet your needs

- Parking large sums of cash into a donor-advised fund without a plan to activate it

PART 3

SUSTAINING THE FAMILY OFFICE

If you've followed my advice so far, your family office principals are well educated and involved in the family office's creation and management, and your office itself is up and running. It should be supporting the family at this point, providing the unique services they need—from investing to bill payment and everything in between.

But that's not the end of the story—not by far. What—you think impressive legacies that last generations come easy? The family office is not a one-off project that you can set up, sit back, and forget about. It is a living, evolving enterprise, and you'll need to evolve with it in order to keep it working. There are some predictable phases that most family offices roll through, such as when the G2 comes of age to participate in the family office and when G1 formally relinquishes control of the family fortune to the subsequent generations. Understanding which phase you're in can help you plan and make decisions about the future of the office.

Speaking of the future, we all need to think about ours. At some point—usually when we least expect it—your accumulated wealth will pass beyond your control. To properly achieve our vision and legacy (as well to avoid chaos, infighting, and potential litigation), we must plan for that eventuality—early and thoroughly. Like every other part of wealth management, the estate plan will evolve over time to reflect your desire to pass down or give out your assets.

Finally, the family office will eventually need new leadership if it is to continue for generations into the future. This means preparing the next generation—or spouses, siblings, or other members of the current generation—to take over when necessary. It means encouraging their involvement in decision-making for the office and ensuring a solid, unbroken succession of leadership. The new leadership may choose to continue with the office as it is, but more likely they will choose to change it to suit their needs or create their own; whichever path they choose, you will have given them the tools to be successful.

CHAPTER 12

Phases of the Family Office

Continuous learning and improvement is required to manage and sustain the family office. You are never done creating, managing, and improving it. In fact, if you feel you are done, then you may in fact be done for. The supply and demand of the family office are constantly changing. The demand, the needs of family members, will shift with each individual and with the changes in their lives and situations. The supply, the type and sophistication of the service providers community, is also constantly in flux. Because these elements are always evolving, so should the family office.

Sometimes this adaptation will be in the form of a few tweaks—swapping out a mid- or lower-level employee for another one, upgrading the cybersecurity protocols, adding a new trust to the mix. Sometimes it will be a more material shift—upgrading the mission statement, changing the board or the CEO of the family office, swapping out a major service provider such as the accounting firm for another. You'll need to have the right mental model about this. Avoid the trap of thinking you are done and that the office can go on autopilot. As with any other high-performing business, there is no such thing as being done in building a family office. The office might be better thought of as a living, breathing work of art; it can be beautiful, but it also needs to constantly adapt. Every once in a while, a big upgrade or even starting from a blank slate may be necessary. Again, like any business, your mindset for the family office should be that of continuous improvement.

Looking Ahead

It's important to keep up with the trends, both internally and externally. Internally, the family is a living and growing entity, and in larger families, this change is hard to keep up with. Beyond simply an individual turning twenty-one or another member getting married, individuals' knowledge of the family office content is, hopefully, growing. Externally, new practices are emerging all the time; new service providers are always getting into the family office market. For every planned-for event which impacts the office, there is usually an unplanned event that needs to be taken into consideration and managed.

Family office networks have played a key role in helping me build a network of other trusted family office principals that I can call on. This has been invaluable. They help surface important trends relevant for family offices and have also introduced me to a variety of third-party professionals. They can also be a source of knowledge in many other ways, such as the stages of growth and planning for the family office. As you benchmark with other family offices, it may be helpful to think about what appear to be some general groupings of the family office in terms of its overall maturity.

In the first phase of a family office, G1, the founder, stands up and runs the office and makes most, if not all, of the major decisions. They tend to be internally focused, with the main purpose of protecting and growing the wealth they've accumulated. They focus on investment management and will usually set up the basic functions of the family office—bill pay, taxes, estate planning.

In the second phase, usually when the second generation takes over the office, you'll see one principal take on the role of CEO, and G1 move to a chairperson role. The office will broaden its constituents to include more generations and may expand the definition of family to include in-laws and partners. It's important to revisit the purpose of the office at this stage to ensure it still fits for all of the principals. This stage will be focused on investment management across different parties with different goals, as well as estate planning, and you'll need to ensure vertical coordination between parents and the next generation.

Finally, the third phase, for those fortunate to make it here, usually coincides with G3's ascension, and a G2 moves into the role of chairperson with less day-to-day involvement in the family office. This stage may involve hefty horizontal coordination across cousins. The goals at this stage are often quite external, such as creating a societal impact beyond the family's sustained wealth. Often, at this stage, the office is managing sizable philanthropic activities as well and may have robust ESG and impact investing programs and investments.

Of course, not all family offices fit on this spectrum. Those offices that are still connected to an operating company may also differ from the stand-alone offices, going through phases at a different pace. These phases can help you determine what you might need at this moment for your family office, but remember that it will continue to evolve.

Table 12.1. Family Office Maturity Framework

	PHASE I	PHASE II	PHASE III
Leadership	G1	G2	G3 and beyond
Role of patriarch or matriarch	CEO	Chairperson	Legacy (trying to convey a passive role of influence, but they are typically not alive by this time)
Purpose/goals	Internally focused; protect and grow wealth; set up initial office	Broaden constituents; revisit purpose	Often quite external—broaden societal impact and create legacy
Key activity	Investment management	Estate planning	Philanthropy
Opportunities	Set professional tone; build great team; stay flexible with outsourced talent as appropriate	Refine providers; rebalance in-house versus outsourced; build consensus with additional principals	Full suite of services; several opportunities for principal involvement
Challenges	Finding the right people for key functions—investment, estate planning, taxes, bill pay, etc.	Vertical coordination between parents and next gen; the "handover"	Horizontal coordination across cousins who may not have deep relationships

Pruning the Family Office Tree

Not every family office can or even should last for an eternity. In speaking with many family offices that have either downsized or, in some cases, disbanded altogether, I've learned that, at times, this is the best option.

I categorize the signs that your family office may not be built to last into three buckets, which are not mutually exclusive.

In the first case, you family principals want and need substantially different things. You'll remember that consensus is crucial to maintain the function of the family office; once that consensus is no longer feasible, neither is a unified family office. It may be that one member has a complex real estate portfolio requiring a lot of customized expertise, or a member may need support for managing issues related to the family business that other family members are not part of. Philosophically, one member may strongly support sustainable investing, and another may want to achieve maximum financial returns irrespective of how the money is made. A common area of disagreement is that the costs of the physical office space

> There are times when it is best for the family office to disband.

plus the staff for the family office may not be equally useful to each member. If not, then there will likely be pressure to minimize costs by those who are on the outside, while those who utilize the space may want to have top-tier office space. Perhaps a family member wants the family office to have staff that cater to that member's activities in a way that is disproportionate to other members. If the members don't agree on what the baseline activities and investments for the family office are, and how costs are allocated, this may be a sign that a split is warranted.

Another contentious situation is when your family principals bring materially different offerings to the table. This may be in the form of time, money, expertise, or network. For example, one member who works in the family office a lot more than the others, or who brings a lot more capital into the family business than the other members, may feel—and perhaps rightly so—that they are pulling more weight than their counterparts. If the contributions are unequal, as in most any business partnership, there will be tension.

Finally, a potentially huge issue is if the family principals don't get along. This goes beyond typical family squabbles or normal sibling rivalry. In this case, we have family members who don't respect each other, don't trust each other, or simply don't like being in the same room. Maybe there is a longstanding grudge one member carries about who got to run the family business or who received what in the patriarch's estate plan. Maybe intense jealousy based on the success of one member and the lack of success of another member. Being part of a family office requires teamwork and compromise for a greater good. If the members don't like their teammates and don't or can't compromise, it is a recipe for failure.

There are situations where it is appropriate to ask certain members to find another home for the activities that are part of the family office. In a perfect world, to maintain family harmony as much as possible, this may be done in a manner that makes it less about any one or multiple individuals and more about roles and requirements.

For example, with one fifth-generation principal I spoke with, the family office was reaching its capacity to serve the members adequately, and a core group of family members determined that the best way to divide the family was into two groups: those who were active in the family business and those who were not. This is an objective measure and one that was justified, in that the family members still in the business had a different set of requirements than those who were not.

In other situations, a specific member may pull out from the larger office if they see a way to have their needs better met elsewhere. Because these cases are somewhat common, it is in everyone's best interest that the process and timing by which the members may pull out of the office is clearly communicated to everyone involved. For how long can the departing member count on some of the family services to continue— through the next tax cycle, for example, or until the end of the calendar year? Are they permitted to pull their capital out immediately, and if so, what are the ramifications for the other members, who perhaps have leverage based on that capital? Who pays the exit or disbandment fees? What about illiquid assets? If a member pulls out, do all members have to pay fees as part of a sale? It is important to hope for the best but be prepared for the worst and to work with experienced attorneys who have dealt with such issues so that important decisions on the process and timing will be spelled out beforehand. An exit out of the blue can rock the boat too hard and could hurt family relations, not to mention the family office.

Of course, there are many ways that a member may remain partially involved in the family office. They may have some capital in it, or they may be a part of the family foundation but not of other family entities. They may utilize the office for accounting services but not for certain legal work. Again, clarity and communication are key to maintaining family relations and the smooth operation of the family office.

From my interviews of family principals, families get into trouble when they have black or white thinking. For example, either family members are 100 percent in the office, with all their capital and activities, or they are out and completely do their own thing. Creating the flexibility for members to come and go, within reason, into the office's services and into specific coinvested entities is an approach that works in many situations.

My siblings and I determined that it was best for us to split up with respect to liquid capital management; each of us found our own managers. For illiquid assets, they are comanaged, at least currently, until they mature, which, for some, could be decades. We each do our own thing with respect to philanthropy. Certain real estate investments are still co-owned. It is probably the case that some of us would like to be more connected across our investing activity and that others would like to be less connected. We exist in a happy medium for now, and it will likely continue to evolve as the years click by.

WHAT WORKS

- The right mindset: the family office needs proper investment of time, energy, and money if it is to survive, let alone thrive

- Respect for the challenge at hand with generational transitions in particular

WHAT DOESN'T

- Ignoring the warning signs (disengaged principals or outdated structures) that the family office is unsustainable

- Needlessly locking in family principals to structures and investment funds, or creating painful exit scenarios that breed resentment

CHAPTER 13

Estate Planning

Planning for the future is difficult even when it doesn't involve death and money. However, when your family's future is at stake, it is crucial to think far ahead. Your estate and how you will pass on your personal wealth to the next generation—or not—is a crucial consideration. Don't put it off; any of us can meet our end at any moment, and if you haven't planned for it, you are creating even more chaos for your family.

Estate planning is among the most subjective areas of the family office. It involves deeply personal values and tough decisions that blend family, love, finance, and mortality. It is a crucial process, in that decisions have substantial impact on the legacy of the family, its creations, and the members. It is also often one of the most underdeveloped parts of family offices. Many family principals don't spend enough time thinking about life after their passing. It's an unpleasant topic. Many think they are healthier or luckier than they turn out to be. In some cases, family principals are hesitant to think too far into the future, not wanting to confront their mortality and perhaps not having confidence in their children's ability to properly manage wealth. In other situations, the principals have made decisions early on in the process of accumulating wealth, and they have clear rules of thumb they try to adhere to, such as having already decided to give a certain percentage of their wealth to their children and the rest to charity. But those early decisions don't necessarily make as much sense later on as your family's wealth and needs change and as the vision of your legacy—for the family and the world—evolves.

Passing Down

How much—quantitatively and qualitatively—do you want to pass to the next generation? The efficacy of passing wealth directly down through the family will be put to the test as generational wealth transfer begins. It has been estimated that, by the third generation, 90 percent of affluent families lose their wealth.[1] The education and engagement of the next generations, effective governance structures like family constitutions, and strategic tax planning can aid your family office greatly during the estate planning and execution process.[2] The strategies here include trusts, wills, and other vehicles.

> How much—quantitatively and qualitatively—do you want to pass to the next generation?

Michael O. Hartz, of Katten Muchin Rosenman LLP, told me, "I am seeing that many principals are interested in passing wealth to the next generation earlier than was the case a couple of decades ago. There is a realization on the part of the principal that, if they wait until their passing, it might mean that their children may not have the opportunity to enjoy the wealth until they are in their sixties. Also, there is a desire by the older generation to give smaller amounts along the way, to help the younger generation get accustomed to the wealth and as a trial to see how they will handle it. Is the younger generation taking the gift of wealth as a serious responsibility? Are they learning the basics of wealth management, learning about investing and taxes, so they can best manage it? In most cases, this works out well, but in a few, the older generation isn't pleased with how the wealth is handled." If the current principal feels that their offspring might squander their hard-earned wealth, might make rash decisions, or might lose interest in making a contribution through work or philanthropy, then the principal may decide to alter their future giving plans. They may place additional constraints on inheritance or may even change their estate plan entirely.

One technique that I am very grateful for having participated in has been drafting a letter of wishes. I credit my advisory council for introducing me to this idea. This letter is nonbinding but provides the color commentary to what you as the grantor would like to see happen once you pass. It is a complement to a formal estate plan. Your estate plan spells out the legality of who assumes ownership of assets; the letter of wishes speaks to how you'd ideally like those assets to be utilized and enjoyed. In my case, I wrote it to my spouse, my children, my extended family members, and the advisors of the family office.

Bessemer Trust has a helpful overview of what this letter is all about:[3]

1. "Letters of wishes written to trustees can help them stay true to your vision and priorities when making distributions to your beneficiaries.

2. "Letters to family members can help generations of beneficiaries understand your history, the reasons behind your decisions, and the values you hope your family will uphold.

3. "These letters should be written carefully so as not to conflict with trust or other legal documents. Professional advisors can guide and ease the process, helping you create letters that will achieve your objectives now and for many years to come."

The letter of wishes is just one part of a larger plan which is designed and put in place well before it is ever needed in order to help your family when you become unavailable.

Giving Out

When a principal directs some of their estate outward, they can make a chosen impact on the larger world. Many family offices choose to direct their capital toward causes of particular importance and meaning for them.

"Especially in the last five to ten years," Michael Hartz says, charitable giving has increased. "This is in part due to better estate planning with young businesses before they grow substantially and in part to large windfalls for the principal and whatever proportion they have retained but also for the next generation, which may have benefited from receiving shares in a rapidly growing business before the value has increased dramatically.

"When this happens," Hartz continues, "the older generation feels they have already committed funds to the younger one" and feel they can more freely "give outside of the family to important causes they care about." This form of giving is "mostly in the form of a family foundation . . . Principals giving philanthropically at this level tend to favor the foundations." A foundation or giving through the family office allows the principal more control of the investment and the capital, allowing them to donate more flexibly. The foundation along with the family office can also serve as "a great tool to teach younger family members about investing and giving" when the younger generation is welcomed into the foundation or family office and allowed to contribute, learn, and experience them.

Although the use of private foundations for philanthropic giving may be lower for some families who are instead utilizing donor-advised funds, there are other options we may see more of in the future, such as 501(c)4-type organizations and special purpose trusts. Patagonia, the outdoor clothing retailer, serves as a good case study here. The founder, Yvon Chouinard, could have chosen to pass the company to his children, but they didn't want to run it. He could have chosen to sell the company and donate the proceeds to charity, but he wanted to ensure the company wouldn't sell out its values to a new owner. In the end, he chose to transfer the company to a combination of a special purpose trust and a charity, so that the company could continue to operate according to the founding values and also do good in the form of paying dividends to the nonprofit.

Sustainable Giving

Historically, those two options—passing down to children or passing out to charity—have been the most common means of disseminating an estate. However, we do see some level of innovation and a gray zone in between these two options, ways in which principals are creating socially minded investments and utilizing some innovative structures that involve giving capital both down and out at the same time.

Importantly, it is possible to combine the goals of capital growth and preservation with positive impact, and principals can do so during their lifetime, so they can see benefits while they are alive. Many families are doing just that. The two are not mutually exclusive, and given that millennials and Gen Z have a particular interest in social and environmental impact, this approach will become particularly important in the coming decades. As a grantor, you have the potential to direct that capital be given to your children and also direct how that capital is managed before and after it is out of your estate. Selecting charities or even placing capital into a family foundation or DAF is in some ways the easy part of the equation, for me at least—who do you want to give to, how much, and for what use?

Finally, a concept that, as of this writing, has gained traction is the notion of a drawdown foundation. If the return of the giving is creating social good, and the giving happens in a drawn-out manner across many decades, then one might discount the good in the out years and conclude that to maximize the good, giving should happen sooner than later. There is a wonderful book written about an amazing businessperson turned philanthropist, the great Chuck Feeney, called *The Billionaire Who Wasn't*. I have found it helpful in terms of thinking about timing of my own philanthropy—how much to give during one's lifetime versus at your passing.

The lesson here is that, when it comes to estate planning, families can choose to prioritize the sustainability of their office and wealth, the use of that wealth for positive social and environmental impact, or a combination of the two: sustainability of their family's prosperity and the world.

Finish the Job

The only thing worse than a bad estate plan is an unfinished one. There is also no single right estate plan that will work for every family or even necessarily for the same family over time. The estate plan works best if it evolves as the family members gain wisdom on their values, as they better understand the family and larger society they wish to serve with their assets, and as they determine their legacy within the broader world around them. I recommend revisiting the estate plan every five years or so and updating it with any necessary shifts in thinking about goals and strategies.

My father wanted the majority of his wealth to be passed to his children. He and his wife did make various philanthropic donations, but it wasn't a topic of much discussion. His gold, his rules. Who am I to judge?

A complicating factor was that among the assets my father passed to my siblings and me were nonfinancial assets—a family vacation property, some pieces of art, and some commercial real estate. He also put in trust for the benefit of the siblings his primary and secondary residences. I will share how the siblings have managed these assets since my father's passing.

The vacation property is a wonderful family compound that the family enjoyed for several decades. It is currently owned by each G2 family unit, but as those families evolve and their desired utilization of the property does as well, some potentially conflicting desires for the property are surfacing. One sibling desires to undertake a major renovation and invest substantial capital to rebuild the compound for the decades to come. Another sibling is interested in funding modest renovations, and the last sibling is fine with things as they are currently, doing essential repairs only as needed.

Given how infrequently the house is utilized, this misalignment has not to date caused much friction, but it certainly has the potential to. Can a G2 member exit and sell their share? Yes, but it is not clearly specified in the operating agreement at what price that would happen—market rate, market less minority discount, cost? What about tax implications of a partial sale: Who is responsible? It is important to spell out as many possible future scenarios as you can and to gain buy-in from each involved principal. An operating agreement for jointly held family assets should specify an exit plan, a succession plan, and capital calls. The succession plan answers the questions: "What happens if a G2 member passes? Does their interest (and voting rights) pass to their spouse, to their younger generation? Does the younger generation need to be at least twenty-one to vote?" Finally, how will these capital calls, required expenses, discretionary expenses, and so on be decided upon? Is there a voting mechanism?

My father and my mother enjoyed purchasing art over the years, and my father had the foresight to put some of the ownership of the collection in a joint entity for the siblings, so that some of the appreciation was on our watch, so to speak. But when he passed—which no one wanted to think about—what would happen to this collection? We struggled to answer this question.

Sibling 1 would ask, "Hey, what will happen with the family art?"

Sibling 2 would join in: "It's a good question. One day, we will have to figure out how to pass on the pieces."

Sibling 3 would then say, "We can figure out things at the right time."

That is about as far as we got in the planning, and that right time never seemed to materialize. We knew it was an asset we'd someday have the responsibility to manage, but we seemed to not want to get into the details. Doing so would entail thinking about our father's passing.

Michael Hartz says, "Principals might be wise to think of estate planning as a business transaction—something they are often very familiar with—and understand the potential ROI of certain estate planning strategies. When framed in this manner and [as] less of an emotional decision about passing wealth, often the principal can see the wisdom of acting versus waiting or inaction."

All said, in retrospect, it would have benefited the family to have given it more attentive thought. We should have documented the following:

- What is the process for sharing and managing the assets? What would my father have wanted? How did that compare to what the next generation wanted?

- Could the owners of the assets sell? If so, to whom and at what price (if intrafamily)?

- Who would pay the taxes on any sales that might occur?

- What does the operating agreement say?

- Do we follow that agreement or agree that it is outdated? What if it is not unanimous?

- Is it fair to all parties?

- If not, then what?

Enough Is Enough

As it relates to my own estate-planning process, I feel fortunate to have a blank slate to work from, as well as the ability to direct my assets toward multiple beneficiaries, not only my children. Whereas my father had decided to pass the vast majority of his wealth to G2, I am not inclined to precisely follow that model for a few reasons.

I believe that there are many valid competing uses for capital—and passing to the next generation is among one of the paths. I know that directing capital into charities and foundations is of course a great use of capital, and I also believe that building for-profit businesses that create social impact is a key way to scale impact. As such, I intend to allocate capital to all three areas.

Yet, I also believe that passing wealth to the next generation beyond a threshold doesn't provide them with more happiness—it can actually create problems. Warren Buffett has famously said he wants to pass enough to his children that they can do anything but not so much that they do nothing. I believe the amount that is passed, as well as when it is passed, is critical. When I think about the level of wealth I would ideally like to see my own children enjoy, perhaps it is on par with the level I have experienced, but it need not be multiple of that amount. My intuition, research, and speaking with many other family office members have confirmed that there is a point at which enough is enough. Coming up with that number and trying to plan for it are challenging, granted.

According to Tavan Pechet, who ran a family office and is now a consultant for others, one of the most common mistakes wealthy parents make is convincing themselves that a big inheritance will make their heirs happy. Money adds happiness up to a point, but health, people, and purpose ultimately drive happiness (and an inheritance can actually impede those drivers!). If you're not sure you can make rent next month, then money adds a lot of happiness; but better to drive a Toyota full of family and friends than an empty Mercedes.

Estate planning has traditionally been approached from the lens of how to give financial and nonfinancial assets, such as those vacation properties and art. But among the most valuable assets that can be passed down is the family office itself—the structure, team, processes, knowledge. For me, an interesting reframing of my mindset has been shifting from thinking about how much money to give to whom, to thinking about how to pass on a high-functioning family office which has, as one of its activities, growing wealth for the benefit of the next generation and the broader society, and does so for multiple generations. That is the real endgame in my mind.

> Better to drive a Toyota full of family and friends than an empty Mercedes.

In order to make that happen, you'll need to engage the next generation in the family office, ensure they are set up for success in terms of the training and support they receive, and ideally have them be successful in leadership positions. Without the background and knowledge we've discussed throughout this book, they may not have the tools to keep the office viable, and they may fall into the 90 percent of wealthy families who fail to retain wealth beyond a couple of generations.

Fair Is Not Always Equal

My parents did a good job of treating my siblings and me as equals throughout my childhood. My siblings and I had what I'd call healthy relationships, which then extended into our twenties and thirties. In our family, one sibling was running the family business, the other sibling had a different set of interests, and I was running my own businesses I had created outside of the family business. We had vastly different experiences with running businesses and familiarity with finance across the three siblings. All of that probably would not have mattered too much, except for the fact that, as time went on, some of the family assets were gradually passed to us to manage.

First was that family vacation property I mentioned earlier. My father ran out of steam to manage it and quietly passed the torch to us. As the family investment capital grew, that too became an asset that my father didn't have much interest or expertise in (his expertise was in running an operating company), and so that defaulted to my siblings and me. Other family assets were more suddenly left to the siblings to manage upon his death.

And so it was a slow realization for me that my relationship with my siblings was evolving; we were now also business partners. And each of our definitions of business partner was probably quite distinct. As anyone who has been there knows, doing business with family can be . . . complex. Each member brings their unique experiences, expectations, and work styles. I had a pretty clear idea of the types of individuals and firms I chose to do business with and the norms I'd expect from each partner. The same goes for my first sibling: clear expectations and norms but most assuredly a different set, coming from a different industry from me. My other sibling brought a different point of view. One sibling likes to talk things through on a phone call; others like the efficiency of email. Another sibling may need more handholding with unfamiliar concepts, especially if they are not managing a business and desire decisions to be more family oriented than business oriented. All of our different expectations are valid, but they are fairly different. The key is to find a happy medium, where possible. It is important to realize when giving assets to the next gen, when those assets are not easily divisible (vacation property, operating property, art collection, etc.), the implications of one's children functioning as business partners with your gift.

I believe my father, in an effort to treat my siblings and me equally, put all the assets he chose to pass to the next gen in a single LLC, co-owned equally by the siblings. At times, I've wondered about the wisdom of this. Maybe it is better to try one's best to split assets but avoid the inevitable family conflict if you have to work through managing joint assets? My father used the expression "Fair is not always equal," which resonated with me. Maybe passing assets in a way that is not totally equal is still fair. And maybe it is actually better for all parties.

I have seen families where the norm is to pass all assets on equally, and I have seen situations where the assets are less equal, at least on paper—the house to sibling A, liquid investments to sibling B. Of course, many variations on this theme exist too: the assets are passed on but must be sold at the time of G1's passing to the next generation, and one party may choose to buy out the other parties.

All of this is to say that estate planning is complicated and fraught with potential conflict. You'll have to determine the individualized and specific method that meets your personal needs and those of your family in the best way possible. Whatever that is, though, it needs to be done. Don't wait until it's too late.

WHAT WORKS

- Thoughtfully creating an estate plan—and perhaps a letter of wishes—and revising them every handful of years to ensure alignment with your vision

- Determining not only how much to give, but also how to and when

WHAT DOESN'T

- Having no estate plan or an outdated one; in either case, your legacy and family will be hampered

CHAPTER 14

Succession Planning

As I write this, my children are quite young. They won't be in a place to manage or help manage the family office for at least ten years, and I have no idea if that is what they will want to do when the time comes. My goal is to provide them with the opportunity—but not the obligation—to take over at some point. This does raise the prospect that the family office stops after my and my wife's passing, although I am currently exploring ways to sustain it via the use of G3 cousins and nonfamily leadership. The planning we are doing needs to take into consideration the variety of scenarios which may unfold.

Think for a moment how much time and effort CEOs and the board of directors at the largest public companies in the world spend on succession planning. This is the central responsibility of the board—the hiring, developing (and firing, when appropriate) of the CEO and their identified successors. Such companies invest a tidy sum in terms of HR energy, outside specialists, and precious board time. I know this since I was providing such services before starting ONE WORLD in a previous leadership development consultancy I ran. However, in family offices—some of which have similar market caps as public companies—it is not uncommon to see zero succession activity. Let's agree—this makes no sense and is dangerous to the legacy of these assets, and to the family members.

"There is a lot at stake" with family office succession, says Laird Pendleton, cofounder of CCC Alliance, "in terms of relationships and financial considerations. For family members, often the family office is the main—if not sole—means by which they stay connected. It can give the family purpose and strengthen the various relationships when the office is functioning well and meeting everyone's needs. When a member pulls out or the office is disbanded, that can often mean the relationships are frayed or even severed. And, financially speaking, a poor succession process can lead to poor investment returns, which will certainly strain family relationships in and of itself."

Success with Succession

Laird continues, "When we see family offices fracture or completely disband, in the majority of cases it is due to a failed succession plan or no plan at all. In fact, 2022 research by the Wharton Global Family Alliance and a separate study by Northern Trust concluded that two-thirds of single family offices did not have a documented succession plan.

"Conversely, the data from the Wharton Global Family Alliance, which goes back to 2008, consistently shows that high-performing families, as determined by several factors including public market performance, have more robust governance structures, and the most important structure in most cases is the succession plan. So, from personal experience and research, I urge every family office to institute a succession plan, no matter how young and healthy your leaders may be. If you truly want your family office to be sustainable, a succession plan is a must."

The obvious question here is: If succession is so important, why do many family offices lack a plan?

According to Laird, "For a senior generation family member, documenting a succession plan is like updating their estate plan or a colonoscopy. Everyone knows you should do it, but it involves uncomfortable planning, contemplating your mortality, and conjures up images of loss of power and relevance. In my family's case, my grandfather waited until his deathbed to document his succession plan, choosing a son-in-law as his successor in the family office and chair of our operating company. One's deathbed is not the ideal time to be making decisions, and while my grandfather's choice of a son-in-law was, in retrospect, the right decision, the wounds and scars caused by the timing of his decision would, in part, lead to a split in our family office in the next generation. Like many family patriarchs, my grandfather was active in many arenas. He was a self-taught architect who built everything from a cathedral to homes for his children. He was passionate about his art collection, his charities, and politics. I am sure he meant to better communicate his succession plan, but he didn't plan to die rather suddenly at eighty-one. So the timing and communication of the plan to the broad family is vitally important."

> If you truly want your family office to be sustainable, a succession plan is a must.

In the short term, my focus is on building up my spouse's level of expertise in running the family office, moving her from an observer to a board member and, ideally, then to a candidate as a chairperson. I am also working on bringing in some of my siblings and even my nieces and nephews—family members that could play a role, even if only by managing things in an emergency. And there are other advisors and trustees who could ramp up their understanding of my game plan with the family office as well.

Laird continues, "The main challenge is, while you want a family member at the helm or, at a minimum, as a very active board member, you have a limited pool of individuals to choose from. Another factor is that, often, family members may be occupied with other business ventures or simply enjoying their wealth; they don't believe it is important to be involved in a meaningful way. And many times, there are well-intentioned family members who have little or no business or investing expertise, which limits their ability to effectively manage the operation, even at the board level."

Laird continues with an important story to underscore the point: "In 1983 our third-generation family trustees reversed a succession that had been in place for seven years and retracted authority from the fourth-generation CEO. As a result, our family office fractured, and I led a movement to leave and launch a new family office. Soon thereafter I was joined by a cousin and cousin-in-law who led their respective branches. Given our family history, our new SFO was acutely aware of the importance of a well-communicated, documented succession plan.

"In 2008 our family office board sent the family office managers to an off-site to design a succession plan. At the time the three of us were in our early fifties and succession seemed a long way off. We iterated the plan with our board for eighteen months and established timetables, next-generation recruitment, and selection processes. Then in 2016, my cousin-in-law, partner, and dear friend died in a plane crash. The one silver lining of this tragic event was that we had a plan in place. In fact, his successor had been approved by our board one month before my partner's passing. I was surprised and grateful to receive several calls from CCC members who had suddenly lost family office leaders. They not only provided practical, moral, and spiritual support, but every one of them said, 'I hope you have a succession plan!' Those who lacked a plan described the chaos that ensued."

Engaging the Next Generation

Engaging the next generation is a common problem for older generations in family offices. Many G2 and beyond principals enjoy the privileges of wealth and the flexibility to do, in some cases, anything they choose. Especially those who may not be trained in finance see the office as something outside of where they want to spend time and energy. Often-cited techniques to start to engage the principals include involving the family members in philanthropy and creating pilot investment funds in an area of interest or in a specific category of investing, such as early-stage venture capital. The idea is to find a way to catch the eye of the younger generation, to show them that the family office is a means of doing what they want to do and supporting what they want to support, not just a vehicle for sustaining wealth.

According to family wealth consultant and MFO Chief Learning Officer Kristin Keffeler, the older generation often innocently assumes that the younger generation cares—or should care—about the same causes they do. But, of course, that usually isn't the case.

When helping the younger generation take the reins, it is important to help them seek answers to two key questions:

- What causes or problems do I believe are worth prioritizing?
- How would I tackle that cause (e.g., philanthropy, commercial investing in public markets, private markets, impact fund)?

Once those questions are addressed to some extent, enabling the younger generation to learn through putting capital to work is more suitable. They may be paired with another member of the family office—an older relative or an outside professional—to coach (not tell) them how they can approach the issue with their capital. To keep their interest, you'll want to show them what is possible, not dictate their choices.

As Laird puts it, mortal problems with family office succession include a "lack of engagement—family members not wanting to be involved in at least an oversight capacity, who have other interests that pull them from this responsibility, and also believe that the hired executives have it all under control, or conversely that the oversight job is too complicated." Another huge issue is "when the older generation infantilizes the younger generation." This includes "the assumption that they don't know what they are doing or they shouldn't have a voice in suggesting changes; that often doesn't end well." This suggests a transfer of power between equals; we of the older generation should look at succession not as giving something to our children but as helping them take over a job they are well prepared to do—provided you have helped prepare them along the way. "Similarly, the older generation needs to have a dignified path to taper down their involvement when the time is right—either when their own capacities are decreasing with age, [or] when the younger generation has proven it is ready to handle the reins."

Indeed, there many ways to provide educational experiences for the next gen, and the current gen. It is important that the individuals in question see the need for the education, how it will enable them to serve in a new capacity and execute their work more effectively. And ideally, there will be a mindset of continuous improvement, which the older generation can instill through words and actions alike. At any point in time, managing the family office may be heavily focused on managing assets; managing the sustainability of the family office over time is more about managing the skills and capabilities of principals and professionals.

WHAT WORKS

- Carrots, not sticks: find enticing opportunities to engage the next gen (e.g., investing in start-ups) versus trying to require the next generation to be involved (or else!)

- Outlining learning and development plans for each family office principal

WHAT DOESN'T

- Nepotism in the family office: putting family members in roles they are not qualified for; instead, give them the training and support they need to be successful

CHAPTER 15

Conclusion

A family office is a financial tool and a potentially multigenerational support system different from the family business but also similar in many ways. Starting a single family office is much like starting any operating business, but your core customer is the family itself. In order to make the family office last, you have to give it all the attention you'd give to any other business. However, single family office principals need a distinct mindset and management techniques specific to running the family office. You'll need to leverage those similarities to a family business, but you'll also need to manage for the differences from a family business. Basically, you, as the principal, need to see your family office as your own business—filled with possibilities but needing proper care to flourish.

All of the principals will benefit from having the right mindset and thoughtfully investing the office's resources. Also crucial are effective business planning processes such as defining the audience for your family office's services, articulating a purpose for the family office, and identifying the values, along with transparent and evolving governance practices, that will sustain your family office. And don't forget robust succession practices.

In many family offices, direct involvement by the members of the family is too low. Often, there are overlooked opportunities for family office principals who don't work full-time in the family office to leverage its resources in their primary work, creating a win-win situation. Others may have cultures or even explicit protocols that discourage or prohibit additional family members from participating. This is all in the hands of the principals to change—if they want.

All businesses try to achieve profitability and innovation. They seek to create a legacy with their service or among their customers. Successful business owners foster meaning for their employees and serve their customers with purpose. Establishing and maintaining a legacy for their organization helps it thrive, and a purpose-driven workplace attracts and keeps talented people. We all want recognition within our market or community, and we want to make a dent on the world. Family offices are blessed with a substantial base of resources—financial, intellectual, and human—and dedicated professionals can make extraordinary things happen and inspiring legacies come to life.

Family offices, in particular, often have the freedom of a longer time horizon in which to operate. They can forgo short-term gain—which is sometimes at odds with doing the right thing in the long term—to create solutions that benefit a wider audience. They have the freedom to make decisions that will have a positive effect on the world, even if that means it may take longer or be subject to additional risk. With your own family office, you have real skin in the game, with your name on the door, and you can be a visible and influential member of your community. The family business provides opportunities for the family, but you do have to navigate a sliding scale between pure business advantage at one extreme and pure nepotism at the other. Sometimes the scale tilts toward family, and sometimes it must tilt toward pure business. Finding that balance between head and heart can be difficult, but it is crucial.

Finally, as you've read a dozen times by now, the most important thing you can do as a principal to achieve sustainability is to treat the family office as you would other high-performing businesses. Make sure it receives a proper amount of investment, that you hire and continuously develop top talent, that you benchmark and continuously improve, and most important, that you as the principal are aware and active in all that is happening. But what does treating your family office like a high-performance business look like in the real world? The five key elements include the right mindset, mission, structure, talent, and flexibility.

Mindset

The right mindset starts with recognizing the task at hand. Family office principals are a distinctive group of individuals with a large amount of wealth, networks, and other resources at their disposal. With this privilege comes responsibility, specifically the responsibility to understand the basics of business and finance, and to manage their capital in a way that they ultimately care about. Sustainability also requires recognizing the ways in which a family office is similar to and different from family operating businesses in general, and how the roles family members play can look dramatically different in one versus the other.

The right mindset accepts that there will be difficult tasks ahead and that family members may need to build business expertise if they don't have it already. At a minimum, family members should develop enough expertise to know how to hire experts if they don't have the needed expertise themselves.

The right mindset also accepts that starting or rebuilding a family office requires a substantial time commitment. In my case, I devoted at least twenty hours a week for the better part of a year to reorganizing my family office. Other family offices are more complex and will require more time on the part of the principal, especially in the early days.

While some of the necessary components may be a bit dreary, generally speaking, the work presents an exciting opportunity to learn about both the family and its capital in new ways, and to learn new skills needed to succeed. Leveraging the capital and other resources of the family office is a great opportunity for the family members to pursue and support the things they are deeply interested in. After all, it is a customized business entity that can be molded in many ways—including ways that embody the kinds of things the broader family is passionate about. You should not feel constrained by conventional ways of thinking about family offices.

The family will have the right mindset when it can answer all of the following questions in the affirmative:

- Is the family creating an office that reflects the unique needs and resources of the family?

- Is the family making the proper investment in the office—time, money, and emotional energy?

- Do the family members understand the challenge ahead, and that many family offices don't successfully pass to the next generation?

- Does the office help to build relationships among family members and help keep the family together?

If the answer to any of the above questions is no for too long a period of time, then it is time to make changes and mold the family office in a way that best serves the members.

Mission

Once you have agreed to allocate time, energy, and (yes) money to the task of building your family office, you can turn to one of the job's most inspiring parts: deciding on its mission.

Some principals only need the family office to protect and grow their capital. To each his own, but those family offices that have a mission that extends beyond the family and into society tend to be more sustainable. Organizations that have an inspiring mission and orient their operations around that mission do better at attracting talent and staying around over the long term.

What can that mission be? Start by looking at the family's philanthropic work. Almost every wealthy family is active in philanthropy. The philanthropic work they're already doing is a good place to start thinking about the kinds of causes that are close to the family's heart, and that could be formalized into a family mission.

But philanthropy is just a start. It's just one way the family office can make an impact beyond the family members themselves. Sustainable and impact investing is another way, and many family offices report that opportunities around sustainable investing have provided a good way of engaging the next generation.

Family principals should try to answer these questions when formulating the mission:

- Who are all the people and groups that you want the office to benefit with its capital and other resources?
- How can the office support them?
- Are the key members of the family excited and inspired about the mission and to have roles in the office?
- What kinds of metrics or outcomes are you going to use to evaluate the performance of the family office?

- How aligned are all family members on the mission? On family philanthropy? On the type of risk and investments that the family is seeking?

Structure

Once a mission is locked in, it's time to think about what needs to be built. The key questions include these:

- What are the key functions that the family office will perform?

- Is the family best served by an MFO or SFO?

- Have we done sufficient analysis around which functions we will insource versus outsource? Can we be world class at what we insource?

- Which family members are going to be involved, and to what extent? Does our structure leverage our principals' expertise and capabilities?

The community of service providers will be an invaluable resource here, as well as benchmarking with other family offices and networking. Keep in mind that the provider community is dynamic and rapidly evolving; you will want to stay current on who does what well. While many principals come into situations where some structure is already in place, it is worth an audit of sorts to ensure that the structure is efficiently serving the mission, and to let go and update pieces of the structure which may no longer have a place in your optimal design.

Talent

Every successful business thinks strategically about talent. In addition, most families hope their children will maintain good relationships with each other in the future. The family office can provide several mechanisms for that. Many family members who participate in a family office end up deriving a lot of personal satisfaction from the experience. But having the right talent doesn't just happen. It takes planning and time.

There are many examples of successful practices to cultivate, attract, and retain family talent.

The key factors to consider are these:

- What skills, bandwidth, and motivation does each family member bring today?

- How will those skills, bandwidth, and motivations evolve in the future—both among the older generations who are retiring and the younger generations who are coming into the family office professionally?

- What's the best way of developing family talent and complementing that talent with outside professionals?

- Is there a formal, detailed, transparent succession plan? We know that having one is highly correlated with a sustainable family office.

Flexibility

Family offices are well served to embrace change and to get in the habit of constantly refining and refreshing current strategies. If those strategies aren't working, make the required changes. In Silicon Valley, we call this a "pivot" and they are often celebrated, not a sign of being on the wrong track. They show that you are wide awake—ojos abiertos, right, Dad? Being entrepreneurial requires taking steps forward even without perfect information. There is a lot of building the wheels while the car is already speeding down the highway—get comfortable with that. Have a plan, compare performance to goals, engage the family in an open and honest way, and then make tweaks. It is important to distinguish what is urgent from what is important, and to allocate resources appropriately. Here are some key questions to ask:

- What is working and what is not? What should we change?
- Are our mission and vision still valid? Does the next generation get excited about them?
- Is it time to redefine who is considered family for our office?
- Is it time to redefine what services are offered via the office?
- What trends and innovations are other family offices pursuing? Which make sense for us?

It is likely that mission, vision, and values don't change that much over the years, but the way that your family brings them to life will—via different structures, different partners, and family members playing different roles as their own lives unfold.

The entire purpose of a sustainable family office is to support the family, and its hopes and dreams in terms of broader societal impact.

In the same way I benefited by having the opportunity to join the family business that my father started, I am highly motivated to create something that my descendants want to be part of. It's my desire that my wife and children have the opportunity—but not the responsibility—to be involved. The responsibility falls on me to make it something that the broader family feels excited and empowered to be part of.

I am honored you took the time to read this book cover to cover (or . . . perhaps just skip to the conclusion). Either way, my hope is that you will evaluate the ideas, tools, and examples in context of what matters for you, your family, and the unlimited potential that you have to create a multigenerational legacy as you build a sustainable family office.

Acknowledgments

I am most grateful for the collaboration and support from the following individuals along the journey of creating this book.

ONE WORLD Advisory Council

Marjorie Brans
Bulbul Gupta
Dan Kalafatas
Tavan Pechet
Laird Pendleton

ONE WORLD Teammates

Sophia Corning
Angie Mertens

Book Contributors

Raphael Amit

Tom Boyden

David Bradley

Josh Cohen

Merial Currier

Jed Emerson

Jake Farver

Catherine Crystal Foster

Frank Ghali

Paige Goepfert

Ryan Harris

Michael Hartz

Kristin Hull

Josh Kanter

Kristin Keffeler

Laura Lauder

Mazyar Mortazavi

Peter Moustakerski

Justin Rockefeller

Stephanie Cohn Rupp

Steve Schwarz

Joel Solomon

Liza Truax

Kelly Zurek

Greenleaf Publishing Team

Matthew Baganz

Erin Brown

Gwen Cunningham

Neil Gonzalez

Jen Glynn

Madelyn Myers

Pam Nordberg

Aaron Teel

Nathan True

Marketing Specialists

Lori Ames

Kevin Hirshorn

Reviewers

Bernadette Clavier

Ben Lester

Christopher Liguori

Deane Malott

Catherine Ross

Ronald Saslow

Brian Thomas

And a special thank you to my wife and children for your support—
¡Las tres nenas!—and for your encouragement.

Family Office Playbook

The following is an excerpt from the *Family Office Playbook*, which the author uses to align the ecosystem of individuals and firms that collaborate on his family office, as well as bring important information and data together under one cover.

Family Office Playbook Contents

I. Mission

- Mission Statement
- Vision - Graphical depiction of what the office looks like today; what it will look like in the future
- Strategy - Outline the unique ways in which the entity will meet its goals
- Goals - 1/5/10 year

II. Operations

- Services - What are the key services that the office delivers, to whom, and how is that going?

- Structure - What does the infrastructure look like? How many entities of what type; how are they connected?

- Team
  › List of key internal and external people
  › Key points of governance
  › Service provider review template (see below)

- Service Provider Review Template

KEY DELIVERABLES	MEASURES OF SUCCESS	RATING (1-10)
(Outline top 4-5 deliverables, 1 or 2 sentences for each	What objective measures or criteria will be used to determine if delivery was successful?	Rating for each deliverable, 1 is terrible, 5 is average, 10 is world class

- Calendar-Table of key filings and requirements throughout the year—see below

MONTH	ITEM	NOTES
January	Top items in each month - IRS filings, key reviews with providers, quarterly meetings for broader family office	Open items from last time, outstanding questions to be addressed, etc.

- Trusts & Entities

  › Entity chart - see below

LEGAL NAME ENTITY/FEIN	DESCRIPTION/ASSETS	TRUSTEES	STATE OF INCORPORATION

- Assets

  › Asset Distribution Graphic (see below sample)

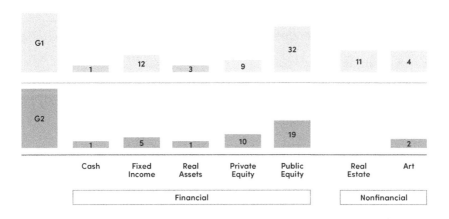

- Tax Filings – see below

LEGAL NAME ENTITY/FEIN	TAXES DUE - AMOUNT PAID	STATE OF INCORPORATION
XYZ Corporation	6/1/2023 $72,000.00	DE

- Insurance
  - › List of key policies - personal and business; see below

POLICY AGENT/INSURER	RENEWAL DATE/ PREMIUM	NOTES
Abbott Trust Homeowners Policy Marsh/Chubb	8/18/23 $15,000.00	Per Marsh - will seek competitive quotes in January of 2025

- Cybersecurity
  - › What are the key activities that are part of the cyberplan?
  - › Who is the main provider?
  - › Chart of endpoints and software installed
- Family Foundation
  - › Purpose
  - › Inception date
  - › Trustees/officers
- Annual tax filing - Accounting firm
- Periodic Information filings - Legal firm

2024

Philanthropy

- Grantee 1 - $X
- Grantee 2 - $X
- Grantee 3 - $X
- Total - $

III. Sustainability Plan

- Estate Planning
    - › What is the layman's version of what the current estate calls for?
- Talent Plan
    - › For each key internal member—principals and executive staff—what skills today/future/development plan

STRENGTHS	GAP ANALYSIS	DEVELOPMENT PLAN
For each key individual, what are they good at?	Per individual and their desired path in the family office, what are areas which can be improved?	What specific items will build the desired skills? · Activities · Courses · Reading · Conferences

- Letter of Wishes
    - › Complements the estate planning; outlines grantor's wishes and intentions as it relates to gifted assets
- Open Items

Advisory Council Overview

The following is an excerpt from the overview document used to describe the Family Office Advisory Council described in the book.

ONE WORLD Mission and Goals

ONE WORLD Investments, Inc. ("ONE WORLD") is the umbrella organization of multiple social impact entities, including the family office activities and assets of (name) and immediate family. ONE WORLD was created as a distinct entity with a distinct mission to "enable organizations to scale social impact and improve the lives of individuals globally."

The problem ONE WORLD is addressing is that the world desperately needs the private sector to address systemic problems, yet the vast majority of companies lack sufficient resources to scale social impact in the form of investment, human, and intellectual capital.

By 2030, ONE WORLD will:

- Provide training to 10,000 professionals
- Support 1,000 businesses
- Activate $1 billion in impact investments

Advisory Council's Purpose and Activities

ONE WORLD's mission requires a structure, ecosystem of partners, expertise and capabilities that extend beyond a typical social enterprise, foundation or family office, and as such has an Advisory Council. The purpose of the Advisory Council is to:

- Help shape ONE WORLD's vision
- Provide input into strategy, structure & partners
- Review performance & impact

Topics of conversation include:

- Mission, strategy, and metrics: How will 1W leverage its assets to achieve its mission?
- Ecosystem evaluation: Does 1W Inc. have the right partners in the right roles?
- Reporting: What is the impact financially and socially?
- Evangelizing: How to inspire the larger FO community toward impact?

Primary activities for council members include participation in:

- Annual review (half day, once per year, in-person as appropriate)
- Quarterly reviews (90 minutes, three per year, remote participation)
- Ad-hoc discussions (telephone, Zoom, or email; not to exceed 1–2 hours per month)

Current Advisors (list all)

- (Name): family office expert consultant, family office principal, attorney, corporate trustee
- Future Advisors: a statement on how the Council is trying to grow (e.g., identify additional advisors with Asian or Direct Investing expertise)

Compensation, Term, or Other

- Annual fee plus all out-of-pocket expenses
- Members serve at a minimum for one year; extended as desired
- NDA requested for confidentiality of sensitive material and specifics on ecosystem partner performance

Sustainable Family Office Research

S ustainable Family Offices is a benchmarking study that examines sustainability in terms of organizational resilience and endurance. The study provides family offices the ability to compare their own succession planning and talent development goals, practices, and activities with peer organizations. The following four tables are an excerpt from the larger study, which encompasses data from a wide variety of sizes, structures, and geographies of family offices.

For additional information on the study, please visit:
www.oneworld.investments/benchmark

Figure C.1. Family Office Goals, Philosophy, and Involvement

	Strongly Disagree	Disagree	Neutral	Agree	Strongly Agree
Our family office is as professionally run as an operating business - we set goals, monitor performance metrics, have a talent plan and culture of accountability, etc. Row %	17%	17%	28%	22%	17%
I believe it is important that the family office passes to the next generation Row %	11%	0%	22%	39%	28%
I believe our family office will pass to the next generation Row %	6%	0%	33%	50%	11%
Other family members believe it is important that the family office passes to the next generation Row %	6%	0%	33%	33%	28%
All family members are encouraged to play some role - even if part - time - in the family office Row %	11%	28%	22%	28%	11%
All family members over the age of 25 have some role - even if part - time - in the family office Row %	11%	28%	39%	22%	0%
Spouses of family members are encouraged to be involved in the family office Row %	22%	22%	28%	22%	6%
Spouses of family members are involved in the family office Row %	24%	29%	29%	12%	6%

Figure C.2. Family Office Succession Planning

	Strongly Disagree	Disagree	Neutral	Agree	Strongly Agree
Our family office has a succession plan that outlines who would take over the family office in an emergency, as well as who are the future successors Row %	11%	21%	32%	26%	11%
I know who will lead the family office after this generation Row %	16%	32%	37%	16%	0%
I put in sufficient time and energy to ensure sustainability Row %	5%	21%	32%	37%	5%
Other family members put in sufficient time and energy to ensure sustainability Row %	11%	37%	37%	16%	0%
The succession plan is shared with and input is given from neutral, objective, non-family professionals Row %	21%	21%	32%	26%	0%
Succession planning gets enough time at family office meetings and is led by more than the current head of the family office Row %	26%	26%	37%	11%	0%
Legal & estate experts have outlined steps and implications of a transition from one family office leader to another Row %	11%	16%	32%	37%	5%
We regularly benchmark for purposes of improving our succession planning processes Row %	28%	39%	28%	6%	0%

Figure C.3. Family Office Talent Development

	Strongly Disagree	Disagree	Neutral	Agree	Strongly Agree
The family office management has outlined what talent capabilities it needs to successfully run the organization Row %	11%	22%	50%	11%	6%
The family office management is clear on what level of skills the current management team has, vis-à-vis the required skills for the family office Row %	11%	33%	33%	17%	6%
Based on the required skills and the current skills, there is a talent gap Row %	6%	28%	39%	28%	0%
We are working on training the next generation Row %	0%	13%	27%	53%	7%
The family office works with outside advisors and professionals to build skills and choose successors Row %	7%	0%	27%	53%	13%

Figure C.4. Family Office Development Formats

For the current family office leadership, as well as successors, the following development formats are utilized:

Value	Percent
Leadership development programs at universities	21%
Custom execution education	64%
Executive coaches	50%
On-the-job training	71%
Outside board roles	36%

Family Office Networks

CCC Alliance: Founded in 1994 by two family offices, CCC is an international network of single family offices that supports member families through learning, collaboration, and the sharing of best practices. In a confidential and solicitation-free environment, CCC runs online forums, virtual and in-person events, and facilitates member connections that form a virtuous circle of member support. CCC employs an un-conflicted model and accepts no form of sponsorship or fees from the provider community and is still owned by their founding families.

Web: www.cccalliance.com
Contact: cccinfo@cccalliance.com

Forge Community: FORGE is a self-governing peer-to-peer network of single family offices that provides events and education for its members, research insights, and an online platform for families to connect and collaborate. Incubated at Fidelity Family Office Services in 2011, FORGE became a wholly owned subsidiary of Fidelity Investments in 2019 and is FORGE's corporate sponsor.

Web: www.forgecommunity.com
Contact: info@forgecommunity.com

Family Office Exchange (FOX): FOX was founded in 1989 and connects families, family office professionals, advisors, and service providers to facilitate learning, collaboration, and mutual support, while providing educational events, consulting, and industry research for its members.

Web: www.familyoffice.com
Contact: info@familyoffice.com

Family Office Real Estate Institute (FORE): Designed for family offices, family members, and family office professionals, FORE specializes in real estate and provides education, research, and a network for collaboration, education, deal flow, and learning from industry experts.

Web: www.fore.institute.home
Contact: info@fore.institute

The Coalition for Impact (C4i): C4i is a global network of networks consisting of family offices, foundations, and other wealth holders and is geared toward promoting positive change and an inclusive financial system through impact investing.

Web: www.coalitionforimpact.org
Contact: c4i@bmw-foundation.org

The Family Wealth Alliance: The only B2B membership organization designed specifically for North American multifamily wealth firms, the Family Wealth Alliance promotes networking and education, facilitates partnerships and collaboration, and provides industry research and thought leadership.

Web: www.familywealthalliance.com
Contact: info@fwalliance.com

Institutional Investor Forums—Family Office Wealth Conference: An annual gathering of family members, single family office executives, and fund managers, the Family Office Wealth Conference covers a wide range of topics from macro conditions, family governance, sustainability, health care, and more. Formats include presentations, working groups, family-only sessions, and workshops.

Web: iinow.com/institutional-investor-forums
Contact: sorted by geography on website

The ImPact: A global membership network of high-net-worth families who are dedicated to managing and directing their assets in a way that aligns with their values and promotes positive social and environmental change around the world. The ImPact supports members through education, events, and collaboration.

Web: www.theimpact.org
Contact: info@theimpact.org

Ultra High Net Worth Institute: An independent nonprofit think tank geared toward educating and empowering its UHNW members and fostering meaningful relationships and collaboration among families and family offices. The Institute hosts events and forums throughout the year and provides an online resource library and discussion board to facilitate learning and mutual support.

Web: uhnwinstitute.org
Contact: info@uhnwinstitute.org

Further Reading

- *The Billionaire Who Wasn't: How Chuck Feeney Secretly Made and Gave Away a Fortune* by Conor O'Clery

- *Complete Family Wealth: Wealth as Well-Being* by James E. Hughes Jr., Susan E. Massenzio, and Keith Whitaker

- *The Cycle of the Gift: Family Wealth and Wisdom* by James E. Hughes Jr., Susan E. Massenzio, and Keith Whitaker

- *The Everything Guide to Investing in Your 20s & 30s* by Joe Duarte

- *The Family Office: A Comprehensive Guide for Advisers, Practitioners, and Students* by William I. Woodson and Edward V. Marshall, part of the Heilbrunn Center for the Graham and Dodd Investing Series

- *Family Trusts: A Guide for Beneficiaries, Trustees, Trust Protectors, and Trust Creators* by Hartley Goldstone, James E. Hughes Jr., and Keith Whitaker

- *Family Wealth: Keeping It in the Family* by James E. Hughes Jr.

- *Global Family Office Investing: Exploring the Practices of Single- and Multi-Family Offices* by Chad Hagan

- *How to Build a High-Performing Single Family Office: Guidelines for Family Members and Senior Executives* by Russ Alan Prince and Robert Daugherty

- *The Myth of the Silver Spoon: Navigating Family Wealth & Creating an Impactful Life* by Kristin Keffeler, MSM, MAPP

- *Principles of Sustainable Finance* by Dirk Schoenmaker and Willem Schramade

- *The Psychology of Money: Timeless Lessons on Wealth, Greed, and Happiness* by Morgan Housel

- *Real Estate Investing for Family Offices: The Family Office Guide to Investing in Commercial and Investment Real Estate* by DJ Van Keuren

- *Succession Planning: Promoting Organizational Sustainability* edited by Pamela A. Gordon and Julie A. Overbey

- *Wealth 3.0: The Future of Family Wealth Advising* by James Grubman, Dennis T. Jaffe, and Kristin Keffeler

- *Wealth of Wisdom: The Top 50 Questions Wealthy Families Ask* by Tom McCullough and Keith Whitaker

- *Women with Money: The Judgment-Free Guide to Creating the Joyful, Less Stressed, Purposeful (and, Yes, Rich) Life You Deserve* by Jean Chatzky

Glossary

A

Accredited Investor: an individual who is authorized to invest in unregistered securities by virtue of income level, net worth, professional experience, or other criteria. An investor must satisfy one or more of the following criteria: an average yearly income of $200,000 annually ($300,000 with a spouse or domestic partner) for the last two years; a net worth over $1M (individually or jointly with a spouse); a profession in the financial sector or achievement of certain certifications and designations.[1]

Accrued Revenue or Expenses / Accrual Basis: accrued revenue or expenses are those which have been earned or incurred without the formal exchange of cash. Accounting performed on an "accrual basis" uses this method.[2]

Actively Managed Accounts: actively managed investment accounts are monitored directly, with trades occurring more often than passive accounts, which often track indices. The former are used in an attempt to maximize returns but can bear greater risks and typically have greater costs than passive accounts.[3]

Investment Advisers Act of 1940: under this federal law, all investment advisors must act according to the fiduciary standard, which includes the duty of loyalty and duty of care, meaning the advisor must act in the best interests of their client(s).[4]

B

Basis Points (bps): used to measure percentage changes in the financial sector for instruments, indices, or benchmarks. One hundred basis points equals 1%, 50 basis points is 0.5%, etc.[5]

Beneficiary: an individual who is legally assigned some benefit, such as an inheritance, an insurance policy, or other assets.

Broker Dealer: an individual or firm responsible for buying and selling securities, either for their own benefit or for the sake of their clients.[6]

C

Capital Gains: an increase in the value of a capital asset (i.e., property and certain intangible investments) that is realized once the asset is sold.

Capital Gains Rate: the rate at which capital gains are taxed once they are realized. Federal capital gains taxes are incurred at a lower level than personal income, while at the state level, these two may be equivalent.[7]

Cash Basis: a method of accounting that only establishes revenues and expenses based on the actual receipt or payment of cash (as opposed to accrual accounting).

Creditor: an individual, organization, or country to whom a debt or obligation is owed.

D

Discretionary Account: an investment account that enables an authorized broker to buy and sell securities on behalf of the account holder without explicit authorization for every trade.[8]

E

Estate Tax: the tax applied to an inheritance whose value exceeds a certain threshold. Taxes are only levied on the portion of the estate that surpasses this "exclusion limit." In 2024, federal taxes are levied on estates worth $31.61M or more and max out at 40% plus a base tax.[9]

F

Family Office Rule (2011): precludes family offices from being categorized as "investment advisers" and therefore eliminates the need for family offices to register with the SEC. These offices must meet several requirements in order to qualify for this exclusion; for example, they must be owned by family clients and controlled by family members.[10]

Fiduciary: any person or organization that is required by law to act in the best interest of their client(s) (i.e., the fiduciary duty) when making financial decisions. Examples include registered investment advisors (RIAs) and trustees.[11]

G

G1, G2, G3, etc.: the consecutive generations of a family office, with G1 referring to the original wealth creators and founders of the office.

H

Haircut: another term for discount applied to an asset's worth. For example, if an asset is thought to be worth $100, but it needs to be sold in a rapid manner or there may be only a fraction of the asset being sold, one may apply a haircut to the value in coming up with the asset price.[12]

Hedge Fund: an actively managed limited partnership that is only available to private, accredited investors and which often uses risky strategies to achieve above-average returns.[13]

HNWI: high-net-worth individual; someone with liquid assets of $1M or more; as of 2024, there are over 5.5 million people in the US at this level.[14]

I

Illiquidity Premium: the additional return an investor receives by allocating capital to illiquid assets (those that cannot be sold and turned into cash quickly or easily).[15]

Institutional Investor: a company or organization (registered investment advisors, insurance companies, pension funds) that invests for their clients.[16]

Investment Policy Statement: a document that provides a comprehensive description of an investor's financial goals, strategies, and preferences and details the responsibilities of the portfolio manager(s), board members, and other relevant parties.[17]

L

LLC: limited liability company; a business structure that protects owners from personal responsibility for the business's debts; a commonly used business entity to hold assets—financial, home, property, etc.[18]

LP: limited partner; an investor who contributes financially to a business or venture for a stake in its profits but has limited voting power and no influence in its daily operations.[19]

M

MFO: multifamily office; an entity that supports several different family offices in their investment, estate planning, tax-related, and philanthropic endeavors, in addition to other services (as opposed to an SFO or single family office).[20]

O

Ordinary Income: individual or business income taxed at a marginal rate; these include wages, salaries, rents, royalties, short-term capital gains, etc.[21]

Ordinary Tax Rate: the tax rates levied on ordinary income.

P

Private Equity: refers to the asset class that includes companies and funds which are not publicly traded, and therefore illiquid. The asset class includes venture capital, which focuses on early-stage private companies, and growth equity for later-stage companies, which may go public in the future. This asset class is generally only accessible to institutional and accredited investors.[22]

Private Trust Company: a state-regulated organization that provides fiduciary services for a specific trust or group of trusts for a family.[23]

Prudent Investor Rule: codified under the Uniform Prudent Investor Act of 1992, this rule stipulates that fiduciaries must act in the best interest of the beneficiaries when managing their assets and should consider diversification, limiting fees, income generation vs. capital appreciation, among other concerns.[24]

Q

Qualified Investor: a status granted to an individual or family with an investment portfolio valued at $5M or greater and which allows access to a wider range of investment opportunities than those available to accredited investors.[25]

R

RIA: registered investment advisor; an individual or firm that provides investment management or services or advice, is registered with the SEC or state securities administrators, and is held to the fiduciary duty.[26]

Risk/Reward: a ratio that denotes the amount of returns an investor can expect to generate for every dollar they risk by investing.[27]

S

SFO: single family office (family office that serves only one family).

SMA: separately managed account; a type of pooled investment vehicle in which an investor owns all of the securities in the account and which thus grants the investor a greater degree of control and transparency.[28]

T

Time Value of Money: the concept that money today is worth more than that same amount of money in the future.[29]

Trustee: an individual or firm that manages or invests assets or property on behalf of a beneficiary.[30]

V

Venture Capital: a subset of private equity that focuses on investing in small, early-stage companies that are not listed on public exchanges. It is one of the riskiest asset classes and also has long-term potential for outsized returns.

Notes

Introduction

1. Josipa Majic Predin, "The Rise and Rise of the Family Office: An Analysis," Forbes, January 11, 2024, https://www.forbes.com/sites/josipamajic/2024/01/11/the-rise-and-rise-of-the-family-office-an-analysis/?sh=6ffac32512ed

Chapter 1

1. "Sustainable Family Office Benchmarking Study," 2023, Question #12, https://www.oneworld.investments/benchmark

Chapter 4

1. Andrew Lisa, "Great Wealth Transfer: How Baby Boomers Are Passing on Fortunes to Heirs," GOBankingRates, June 5, 2024, https://www.gobankingrates.com/money/wealth/the-great-wealth-transfer-how-baby-boomers-are-passing-on-fortunes-to-heirs/ https://www.nasdaq.com/articles/the-great-wealth-transfer%3A-how-baby-boomers-are-passing-on-fortunes-to-heirs

Chapter 5

1. Morgan Stanley Single Family Office Compensation Report 2023, https://www.morganstanley.com/articles/single-family-office-compensation

2. Pooneh Baghai, Olivia Howard, Lakshmi Prakash & Jill Zucker, "Women as the Next Wave of Growth in US Wealth Management," McKinsey & Company, July 29, 2020, https://www.mckinsey.com/industries/financial-services/our-insights/women-as-the-next-wave-of-growth-in-us-wealth-management

3. "Tradition, Trust, and Time: The Challenges Women Breadwinners Face Embracing Their Financial Clout," UBS, 2023, https://www.ubs.com/content/dam/assets/wm/static/doc/own-your-worth-pp-ada.pdf

4. Gustav Tinghög, Ali Ahmed, Kinga Barrafrem, Thérèse Lind, Kenny Skagerlund, and Daniel Västfjäll, "Gender Differences in Financial Literacy: The Role of Stereotype Threat," *Journal of Economic Behavior and Organization* 192 (December 2021): 405–416, https://doi.org/10.1016/j.jebo.2021.10.015

5. "Tradition, Trust, and Time," UBS.

6. "Women on Purpose: Values, Money and the Pursuit of More Intentional Lives," UBS, May 13, 2022, https://www.ubs.com/us/en/wealth-management/who-we-serve/specialized-advice/women-and-finances.html?campID=SOME-OYW2023-GLOBAL-ENG-LINKEDIN-UBSCORPORATE-ANY-ANY-20230613-IMAGE-ALLFOLLOWERS-ORGANIC&sprinklrpostid=100004239361700

Chapter 7

1. David Struthers and Francois Botha, Family Office Software and Technology in 2023, Simple, October 2023, https://andsimple.co/reviews/family-office-software/

2. UBS, Global Family Office Report 2023 (Zurich: UBS Switzerland AG, 2023), https://www.ubs.com/global/en/family-office-uhnw/reports/archive.html

3. Simple, Family Office Software and Technology in 2023.

4. Campden Wealth, North America Family Office Report 2022 (London,

UK: Campden Wealth Limited, 2022), https://www.campdenwealth.com/
sites/default/files/GFO_NA_2022_D.pdf

5.   BlackRock 2022–2023 Global Family Office Report, BlackRock Inc.,
     January 2023.

6.   Simple, Family Office Software and Technology in 2023.

7.   "Cybersecurity Within Your Family Office," Eisner Amper,
     Feb. 22, 2022, https://www.eisneramper.com/insights/real-estate/
     cybersecurity-family-office-0222/

8.   UBS, Global Family Office Report 2023.

9.   UBS, Global Family Office Report 2023.

10. Forge Community, "Benchmarking Survey Report: Costs of Running
     a Family Office" (2021), https://www.forgecommunity.com/-/media/
     project/forge/2020-forge-cost-of-running-a-family-office-report.
     pdf?la=en#:~:text=The%20overall%20average%20cost%20ratio,t%20
     tell%20the%20whole%20story

11. "What Does It Cost to Run a Family Office?," Simple, updated January 16,
     2024, https://andsimple.co/insights/family-office-costs/

12. GreenLock, "Unpacking Investment Fees: A Guide for Family Offices,"
     Simple, updated January 16, 2024, https://andsimple.co/insights/
     family-office-investment-fees/

Chapter 8

1.   UBS, Global Family Office Report 2023.

2.   Adam Hayes, "Volatility: Meaning In Finance and How It Works with
     Stocks," Investopedia, March 31, 2023, https://www.investopedia.com/
     terms/v/volatility.asp

3.   Emily Steinbarth and Bin Wang, "What Investors Need to Know About
     the Surge in Interest Rate Volatility," Russell Investments, June 12, 2023,
     https://russellinvestments.com/us/blog/interest-rate-volatility-surge; Rachel
     A. Rasmussen, "What Is Volatility and Is It Normal?," Foster and Motley,
     February 20, 2019, https://www.fosterandmotley.com/insights/2019/02/20/
     what-is-volatility-and-is-it-normal#:~:text=The%20graph%20below%20
     shows%20historical,rises%20and%20falls%20over%20time

Chapter 9

1. BlackRock 2022–2023 Global Family Office Report.

2. Citibank, Global Family Office Survey Insights 2023, https://www. privatebank.citibank.com/newcpb-media/media/documents/global-family-office-report-2023.pdf

3. Campden Wealth, North America Family Office Report 2022.

4. McKinsey & Company, Private Markets Turn Down the Volume: McKinsey Global Private Markets Review 2023, March 2023, https:// www.mckinsey.com/~/media/mckinsey/industries/private%20equity%20 and%20principal%20investors/our%20insights/mckinseys%20private%20 markets%20annual%20review/2023/mckinsey-global-private-markets-review-2023.pdf

5. UBS, Global Family Office Report 2023.

6. Citibank, Global Family Office Survey Insights 2023, https://www. privatebank.citibank.com/newcpb-media/media/documents/global-family-office-report-2023.pdf

7. Hugh MacArthur, Rebecca Burack, Graham Rose, Christophe De Vusser, Kiki Yang, and Sebastien Lamy, "Private Equity Outlook 2024: The Liquidity Imperative," Bain and Co., March 11, 2024, https://www.bain. com/insights/private-equity-outlook-liquidity-imperative-global-private-equity-report-2024/

8. BlackRock 2022–2023 Global Family Office Report.

9. Campden Wealth, North America Family Office Report 2022.

10. "Venture Capital—Worldwide," Statista, updated March 2024, https:// www.statista.com/outlook/fmo/capital-raising/traditional-capital-raising/ venture-capital/worldwide#capital-raised

11. Neil Patel, "90% of Startups Fail: Here's What You Need to Know About The 10%," Forbes, January 16, 2015, https://www.forbes.com/sites/ neilpatel/2015/01/16/90-of-startups-will-fail-heres-what-you-need-to-know-about-the-10/?sh=319af1826679

12. Simple, Family Office Venture Capital Review 2023, updated July 26, 2023, https://andsimple.co/reviews/family-office-venture-capital/

13. Maureen Austin, David Thurston & William Prout, "Building Winning Portfolios Through Private Investments," Cambridge Associates, August 6, 2021, https://www.cambridgeassociates.com/wp-content/uploads/2021/08/Building-Winning-Portfolios-Through-Private-Investments-2.pdf

14. BlackRock 2022–2023 Global Family Office Report.

15. UBS, Global Family Office Report 2023.

16. David Struthers, Family Office Real Estate Review 2022, Simple, updated July 24, 2023, https://andsimple.co/reviews/family-office-real-estate/

17. Steven Gesis, "An Inside Guide to Family Office Real Estate Investments," Smartland, last updated May 12, 2023, https://smartland.com/resources/an-inside-guide-to-real-estate-family-office-investments/

18. BlackRock 2022–2023 Global Family Office Report.

19. David Struthers, Family Office Real Estate Review 2022, Simple, updated July 24, 2023, https://andsimple.co/reviews/family-office-real-estate/

20. BlackRock 2022–2023 Global Family Office Report.

Chapter 10

1. Morgan Stanley, Sustainable Signals Individual Investors and the COVID-19 Pandemic, 2021, https://www.morganstanley.com/assets/pdfs/2021-Sustainable_Signals_Individual_Investor.pdf

2. Dean Hand, Ben Ringel, and Alexander Daniel, Sizing the Impact Investing Market (New York: The Global Impact Investing Network [GIIN], 2022), https://s3.amazonaws.com/giin-web-assets/giin/assets/publication/research/2022-market-sizing-report-final.pdf

3. Kroll, ESG and Global Investor Returns Study, September 13, 2023, https://www.kroll.com/en/insights/publications/cost-of-capital/esg-global-investor-returns-study

4. Jessica Jeffers, Tianshu Lyu, and Kelly Posenau, "The Risk and Return of Impact Investing Funds," S&P Global Market Intelligence, updated February 23, 2024, https://dx.doi.org/10.2139/ssrn.3949530

5. UBS, 2022 (Zurich: UBS Switzerland AG, 2022), 35, https://www.ubs.com/global/en/family-office-uhnw/reports/gfo-client-report.html

6. UBS, Global Family Office Report 2022, 32.

7. GIIN (website), accessed March 26, 2024, https://thegiin.org/

8. UBS, Global Family Office Report 2022, 28.

Chapter 11

1. Campden Wealth, North America Family Office Report 2022.

2. Laura and Gary Lauder, "Increasing Your Impact by Blurring the Lines between Investing and Philanthropy," LauderFamilyFund.org, March 2022, https://www.lauderfamilyfund.org/four-buckets/

Chapter 13

1. Nasdaq, "Generational Wealth: Why do 70% of Families Lose Their Wealth in the 2nd Generation?", October 19, 2018, https://www.nasdaq.com/articles/generational-wealth%3A-why-do-70-of-families-lose-their-wealth-in-the-2nd-generation-2018-10

2. Francois Botha, "Multigenerational Wealth Transfer: What You Need to Know," Simple, updated October 21, 2022, https://andsimple.co/insights/preserving-multi-generational-wealth-family-offices/

3. Lynn C. Halpern, Jaclyn G. Feffer, and Donna E. Trammell, "Sharing Your Vision and Values: Exploring Letters of Wishes," Bessemer Trust, April 20, 2023, https://www.bessemertrust.com/insights/sharing-your-vision-and-values-exploring-letters-of-wishes

Glossary

1. Adam Hayes, "Accredited Investor Defined: Understand the Requirements," Investopedia, updated October 31, 2023, https://www.investopedia.com/terms/a/accreditedinvestor.asp

2. "Accrual Accounting 101: What Accrued Revenue Is and How to Handle It," Stripe.com, updated March 27, 2023, https://stripe.com/resources/more/accrual-accounting-101#:~:text=Accrued%20revenue%20is%20income%20that,before%20it%20bills%20the%20customer

3. James Chen, "Passive Investing Definition and Pros & Cons, vs. Active Investing," Investopedia, updated December 29, 2020, https://www. investopedia.com/terms/p/passiveinvesting.asp#:~:text=Passive%20 investing%20targets%20strong%20returns,greater%20risks%20than%20 passive%20investment

4. Julia Kagan, "Investment Advisers Act of 1940 Definition, Overview," updated October 28, 2021, https://www.investopedia.com/terms/i/ investadvact.as

5. Chad Langager, "Basis Points: Understanding What They Are and How They Are Used," Investopedia, updated December 10, 2023, https://www. investopedia.com/ask/answers/what-basis-point-bps/#:~:text=Key%20 Takeaways,or%200.0001%20in%20decimal%20form

6. Adam Hayes, "What Is a Broker-Dealer (B-D), and How Does It Work?," Investopedia, updated March 03, 2024, https://www.investopedia.com/ terms/b/broker-dealer.asp

7. "2023 and 2024 Capital Gains Tax Rates," Fidelity, December 21, 2023, https://www.fidelity.com/learning-center/smart-money/capital-gains-tax-rates#:~:text=Short%2Dterm%20capital%20gains%20 taxes,and%2Dlong%20term%20capital%20gains; "Capital Gains Tax," Ballotpedia, accessed March 27, 2024, https://ballotpedia.org/ Capital_gains_tax

8. James Chen, "Discretionary Account: Definition, Examples, Pros & Cons," updated December 15, 2020, https://www.investopedia.com/terms/d/ discretionaryaccount.asp#:~:text=What%20is%20a%20Discretionary%20 Account,documentation%20of%20the%20client's%20consent

9. Julia Kagan, "Estate Tax: Rates, Exclusions, and Impact on Gift and Inheritance Taxes," Investopedia, updated January 18, 2023, https://www. investopedia.com/terms/e/estatetax.asp; Amelia Josephson, "A Guide to the Federal Estate Tax for 2024," Smart Asset, updated December 20, 2023, https://smartasset.com/taxes/all-about-the-estate-tax

10. "Family Office Insights: The Family Office Rule Under the Investment Advisers Act," Squire Patton Boggs, accessed March 27, 2024, https:// www.squirepattonboggs.com/-/media/files/insights/publications/2017/06/ family-office-insights-the-family-office-rule-under-the-investment-advisers-act/26895-2017_june_family-office-insight_-family-office-exemption.pdf

11. Adam Hayes, "Fiduciary Definition: Examples and Why They Are Important," Investopedia, updated March 19, 2024, https://www.investopedia.com/terms/f/fiduciary.asp

12. Cory Mitchell, "Haircut: What It Means in Finance, With Examples," Investopedia, updated June 27, 2023, https://www.investopedia.com/terms/h/haircut.asp

13. Investopedia Team, "Hedge Fund Definition, Examples, Types, and Strategies," Investopedia, updated February 29, 2024, https://www.investopedia.com/terms/h/hedgefund.asp

14. Robert Frank, "The U.S. Is the Top Country for Millionaires and Billionaires," CNBC, March 22, 2024, https://www.cnbc.com/2024/03/22/the-us-is-the-top-country-for-millionaires-and-billionaires.html

15. TJ Porter, "Liquidity Premium: Definition, Examples, and Risk," Investopedia, updated November 07, 2023, https://www.investopedia.com/terms/l/liquiditypremium.asp#:~:text=Liquidity%20premium%20is%20the%20extra,the%20money%20is%20tied%20up

16. James Chen, "Institutional Investor: Who They Are and How They Invest," Investopedia, updated November 22, 2021, https://www.investopedia.com/terms/i/institutionalinvestor.asp

17. Suzanne Lindquist, "The Importance of an Investment Policy Statement," Morgan Stanley, February 17, 2023, https://www.morganstanley.com/articles/investment-policy-statement#:~:text=An%20investment%20policy%20statement%20describes,investment%20committee%2C%20investment%20managers%20and

18. Jason Fernando, "What Is an LLC? Limited Liability Company Structure and Benefits Defined," Investopedia, updated March 21, 2024, https://www.investopedia.com/terms/l/llc.asp

19. Will Kenton, "Limited Partner: What It Is, Laws, Role, and Tax Treatment," Investopedia, updated October 02, 2022, https://www.investopedia.com/terms/l/limited-partner.asp

20. "What Is a Multi-Family Office?" Cresset, accessed March 27, 2024, https://cressetcapital.com/post/what-is-a-multi-family-office/

21. Daniel Liberto, "Ordinary Income: What It Is and How It's Taxed," Investopedia, updated December 11, 2023, https://www.investopedia.com/terms/o/ordinaryincome.asp

22. James Chen, "Private Equity Explained with Examples and Ways to Invest," Investopedia, updated March 13, 2024, https://www.investopedia.com/terms/p/privateequity.asp

23. Rebecca Lake, "What Is a Private Trust Company?," Smart Asset, December 29, 2021, https://smartasset.com/estate-planning/private-trust-company; "Private Trust Companies A Primer," Wealthaven, accessed March 27, 2024, https://wealthaven.com/publications/private-trust-companies-a-primer/; Catherine Moore, "The Use of Private Trust Companies," Ogier, October 3, 2022, https://www.ogier.com/news-and-insights/insights/the-use-of-private-trust-companies/#:~:text=British%20Virgin%20Islands.-,What%20is%20a%20private%20trust%20company%3F,from%20the%20public%20at%20large

24. Adam Hayes, "Prudent Investor Rule: What It Is, How It Works," Investopedia, updated July 12, 2022, https://www.investopedia.com/terms/p/prudent-investor-rule.asp

25. "Qualified Purchaser vs Accredited Investor – What You Need to Know," Yieldstreet, September 1, 2023, https://www.yieldstreet.com/resources/article/qualified-purchaser-vs-accredited-investor-what-you-need-to-know/

26. Adam Hayes, "Registered Investment Advisor (RIA) Definition," Investopedia, updated June 10, 2023, https://www.investopedia.com/terms/r/ria.asp

27. Adam Hayes, "Risk/Reward Ratio: What It Is, How Stock Investors Use It," Investopedia, updated March 03, 2024, https://www.investopedia.com/terms/r/riskrewardratio.asp

28. Rachel Cautero, "How a Separately Managed Account (SMA) Works," Smart Asset, updated April 1, 2022, https://smartasset.com/investing/separately-managed-account

29. Shauna Carther Heyford, "Understanding the Time Value of Money," Investopedia, updated January 30, 2024, https://www.investopedia.com/articles/03/082703.asp#:~:text=The%20time%20value%20of%20money%20is%20a%20financial%20principle%20that,larger%20amount%20in%20the%20future

30. Investopedia Team, "What Is a Trustee? Definition, Role, and Duties," Investopedia, updated February 29, 2024, https://www.investopedia.com/terms/t/trustee.asp

About the Author

SCOTT SASLOW is the founder and CEO of Palo Alto, California-based ONE WORLD Investments Inc., which provides investment capital and advisory services to help organizations scale social impact. ONE WORLD also manages an early-stage impact investing fund. Over his career, Scott has been a founder or founding team member of seven start-up businesses.

Prior to ONE WORLD, Scott was the founder and CEO of The Institute of Executive Development, supporting executives in Global 2000 organizations, including American Express, BlackRock, Intel, Time Warner, and the US Navy. Earlier in his career, Scott worked at Siebel Systems and Microsoft Corporation in leadership roles.

Scott is a graduate of Harvard Business School (MBA) and Northwestern University (B.A., economics). He has authored over twenty-five articles for publications such as *Forbes* and *Directorship* and has been interviewed by and quoted in *Harvard Business Review*, *Bloomberg*, and *BusinessWeek*. Additional information on Scott and his work can be found at www.oneworld.investments

Made in the USA
Las Vegas, NV
12 January 2025

16284857R00146